how to be a better....

communicator

Sandy McMillan

KOGAN
PAGE

The
Industrial
Society

YOURS TO HAVE AND TO HOLD
BUT NOT TO COPY

First published in 1996
Reprinted 1997 (twice)

Kogan Page Limited
120 Pentonville Road
London N1 9JN

© Sandy McMillan, 1996

British Library Cataloguing in Publication Data
A CIP record for this book is available from the British Library.
ISBN 0 7494 2025 1

Typeset by Photoprint, Torquay, Devon
Printed in England by Clays Ltd, St Ives plc

CONTENTS

HOW TO BE A BETTER . . . SERIES

Whether you are in a management position or aspiring to one, you are no doubt aware of the increasing need for self-improvement across a wide range of skills.

In recognition of this and sharing their commitment to management development at all levels, Kogan Page and the Industrial Society have joined forces to publish the How to be a Better ... series.

Designed specifically with your needs in mind, the series covers all the core skills you need to make your mark as a high-performing and effective manager.

Enhanced by mini case studies and step-by-step guidance, the books in the series are written by acknowledged experts who impart their advice in a practical way which encourages effective action.

Now you can bring your management skills up to scratch *and* give your career prospects a boost with the How to be a Better ... series!

Titles available are:
How to be Better at Giving Presentations
How to be a Better Problem Solver
How to be a Better Interviewer
How to be a Better Teambuilder
How to be Better at Motivating People
How to be a Better Decision Maker
How to be a Better Communicator
How to be a Better Negotiator

Forthcoming titles are:
How to be a Better Project Manager
How to be a Better Creative Thinker

Available from all good booksellers. For further information on the series, please contact:

Kogan Page, 120 Pentonville Road, London N1 9JN
Tel: 0171 278 0433   Fax: 0171 837 6348

1

WHAT'S THIS ABOUT?

COULD THIS BOOK REALLY HELP?

Many books assume you do not know anything; they expect you to sit back and take in the wisdom of an expert. This is the view of learning as an essentially passive process. Instead, this book assumes that you already know a great deal, and have a set of skills and experience which is uniquely yours. It also assumes that you are reading it because you hope it will give you something useful and practical to do. The book therefore sets out to help you work out how to use the techniques of effective communication in your own work and life.

It is hard to develop your practical skills through a passive experience, lying back and let the words wash over you; it must be an active and lively process. You will find here many questions and activities for you to try. The book will work best for you if you think about what is going on and set these thoughts down to make your own unique contribution. This all helps with the very real problem of all books – the writer cannot hear what you say, nor find out what you think, nor amend this until it is exactly right for you personally. If you do not want to write in the book itself (a sacrilege to some people!) then get a note pad and keep a record of your ideas.

This participative approach will only work, of course, if the book has something useful for you in it, so we had better start by examining that. You may already have had a look at the Contents page – go back and check it again – looking for things that could help you. What might you get from this book that would be useful? Jot down some ideas here.

If this book is really useful to me, then what I'll get from it is . . .

✎
_____

_____

_____

_____

_____

_____

WHAT WAS THE POINT OF THAT?

I hope you tried that first activity, because it illustrates two major points. Communication only works properly if:

❏ *it has a clear purpose*: if you don't know where you're going then you'll wind up somewhere else (and not even know it);
❏ *it's cooperative*: both sender and receiver must put their brains in gear, or nothing much will happen.

So, if you skipped the activity I would like to invite you to go back and try it. What do you want to get from investing your valuable time and effort into this book? If the answer is 'Not a lot', then maybe you'd be better off doing some other activity which produced some useful and practical result.

BEGIN AT THE END

People sometimes get stuck with what they're doing; that terrible feeling of having tried all the answers you can identify

– but nothing works. 'There must be some way out of here!'. One exit that usually works is to define the clear purpose mentioned above. *Begin at the end* by working out exactly where you want to get to. Once you know that, it is easier to think of ways to get there.

Here are some questions that might help you get unstuck from swamps of communication:

❑ What am I going to get by sorting this issue out?
❑ What is going to be different when I've solved this problem?
❑ What actual results will I see when I have solved this problem?
❑ What exactly do I want people to *know* when I have communicated with them?
❑ What *exactly* do I want people to *do* when I have communicated with them?

You will notice that it says *when*, not *if*. Human beings are resourceful, so I believe that you can work out how to handle your problems: the odds are in your favour.

Often, just making yourself begin at the end will be enough to unstick you from whatever swamp is holding you back. Once you can see where you are going it gets easier to start moving. If this turns out *not* to be enough on its own, then it is still a useful beginning to your journey. More later about how to keep moving forward.

BUT WHY CAN'T I JUST TELL THEM?

It can sometimes feel that you only need to deliver a message clearly to get the result you want, so we need to test how well this one-way method works. Take a moment to make two lists, of successful and unsuccessful attempts to communicate with you, at work or away from it.

Times when someone was trying to tell me something, and it worked – I got the message and accepted it:

✎

_____

_____

_____

_____

_____

Times when someone was trying to tell me something, and it *didn't* work – I rejected or disagreed with the message:

✎ _____

_____

_____

_____

_____

_____

THE COOPERATION SCALE

Table 1.1 shows the Cooperation Scale, which measures how much two-way action a communication has.

Look back at your two lists and give each item a Cooperation Score. There are, of course, many factors affecting whether a communication worked or not. They include the relationship between you, and how tired you were, and whether you wanted

Table 1.1 *The cooperation scale*

Completely cooperative		Completely uncooperative
The other person:	5 4 3 2 1 0	The other person:
❏ seemed to have considered my views		❏ didn't consider my views at any time
❏ asked me what I thought before telling me things	5 4 3 2 1 0	❏ didn't ever ask me anything at any time
❏ listened to what I said	5 4 3 2 1 0	❏ interrupted me or talked me down if I said anything
❏ was interested in getting a result we both could agree	5 4 3 2 1 0	❏ wanted to beat me
❏ spent as much time listening to me as talking	5 4 3 2 1 0	❏ talked all the time and didn't listen at all

to listen to what you were being told. Nevertheless, the chances are good that the successful communications have a higher Cooperation Score than the ones that did not work so well.

If you ignore the other person's views then your communication will probably fail.

CAN ONE-WAY COMMUNICATION WORK?

Common sense suggests that some one-way messages must work, so it would be useful to try working out what they are. This would help you to decide how much you needed to listen as well as talk, and how much mutuality you should build in to a particular communication. Try another two lists to see if this becomes clearer.

I would have to listen to the other person if . . .

✎
_____

_____

_____

_____

_____

_____

I would not have to listen to the other person if . . .

✎
_____

_____

_____

_____

_____

_____

SOME SUGGESTIONS ABOUT TWO-WAY COOPERATION

Unfortunately, I cannot read your ideas, but they probably suggest that you must listen as well as talk if:

❑ you need other people's cooperation or commitment;
❑ people can reject what they are being told;
❑ people might do something that you do *not* want;
❑ the ideas are complex or difficult to understand;
❑ you want people to do 'the right thing' unsupervised;
❑ you want people to change their attitudes or their behaviour;
❑ you want people to learn something new.

There must be important messages you might want to send that do not fit any of these conditions. However, it is hard to think of any.

Generally, though, it is clear that it will *not* be enough simply to think about what you want to tell people. You will have to think about their views if you really want to communicate successfully. Furthermore, you will have to build those views into your planning so that people can hear and accept what you are saying.

Try to avoid beginning 'the dialogue of the deaf".

SUMMARY

In this first chapter we looked at a number of issues:

❑ How can this book be really useful to you? (by building on your skills, knowledge and experience)
❑ Are you ready to invest your ideas and time into it?
❑ *Begin at the end* to get good results (this focuses you and makes every word count).
❑ Making your communications cooperative (to move everyone forward and minimise conflict).

EXPERIMENTS

As an intelligent person, you will want to test whether this book is telling you the truth or only spinning some kind of plausible story. Here are some things to try which should help you to make up your mind.

Does the style of this book work for you?

Find a textbook on communication which concentrates on delivering a clear message (but does not try to involve you in the way this book does). Read the first chapter.

Test the effectiveness of both books by writing down a summary of both first chapters.

Which one did you remember most of?

Do I really want to bother with the rest of the book?

Nobody can answer this one but you – you may not even want to ask the question! One of the marks of your intelligence is that, by and large, you weigh up actions and only do what you want to. Most things are a balance of *rewards* and *penalties*; if you go ahead will you get more sweeties than pain, or the other way around?

Try making a list of both the rewards of working at this book *and* the penalties you'll have to pay if you do.

I hope the balance comes out positive and you stay with us, but if not then you can probably find something else useful to do instead. Good luck!

How much does it help to begin at the end?

Pick a couple of things that you would like to get done next week – not major ones, just ordinary jobs to do. Take the first one and write down some answers to these questions:

❑ What will I get out of doing this?
❑ What will be better when I've done it?
❑ How will I know that I've done it well?

As for the second job, do not do anything special.

At the end of next week, see whether there is any difference in the results of the two jobs.

How much difference does it make to listen as well as tell?

Identify something you have tried to tell somebody recently that did not work as well as you would have liked. There could be many reasons *why* it did not go quite right for you. However, for this experiment concentrate on trying to find out whether the other person felt you were listening or not. If you are feeling brave, you might ask them 'Did you feel I was listening to you when you were telling me about . . .?'

Now try asking 'What was it that you felt I didn't hear properly?' Oh yes, and *listen* to the answer.

Now try again to get your message through, taking account of what the other person has just said to you.

I hope it works; good luck!

2

Making a Start

IT'S ALL VERY WELL, BUT . . .

You may now be thinking 'It's all very well for him to go on about being cooperative, but he doesn't have to cope with some of the awkward people I have to deal with!'

Indeed, what about the awkward, unsharing, unlistening, uncommunicative, difficult people out there? How can you cooperate with an uncooperative person, someone who simply won't help? Why bother, anyway?

What's the point of bothering to get cooperation?

If you and X are having problems with one another, there are three things you might *both* agree to look for:

❏ Something to do that would solve the problem.
❏ Some way of getting the best results for both of you, without either of you having to suffer.
❏ A way to improve your joint ability to solve problems together in the future.

Most people work on intelligent self-interest; I am much more likely to scratch your back if you are already giving me a warm feeling between my shoulder-blades. If we both wait for the other to start then we may both have a long and unscratched wait.

AN EXPERIMENT IN GETTING COOPERATION STARTED

Think of someone, at work or away from it, that you have disagreed with about something. This first time, it might be best to pick a fairly minor disagreement so that it will not be too serious if the experiment does not work.

The chances are quite good that your previous attempts to solve the problem have concentrated on the problem itself. This seems logical, so most of us spend a lot of time trying to get the other person to see our point of view about the problem. There may be a fair amount of 'You shouldn't have . . . ' and 'If only you'd . . .' and 'Don't you feel that . . .' and 'I wish you'd . . .'. You may have noticed that this tends to get you into an argument, but may not move you forward very much. Here is a practical alternative.

What really interests both of you is the *solution*; the problem has already happened. You can only change the future – the past is fixed. If both of you could put your energies into looking for solutions, the problem would stop being important and you could both progress. See if you can get the other person's cooperation so that two heads can be better than one.

Here are some questions to try; keep going as long as you get *Yes* answers.

Can we agree that:

❑ we both want to solve the problem?
❑ whatever we do, both of us must get the best possible results? And neither of us should lose more than the other?
❑ it would help if we work out a practical way of solving mutual problems in future?
❑ this probably means we will both have to be flexible, again without either of us losing more than the other?

If you have got a *Yes* to all of those, the two of you now have a problem-solving agreement. More in a moment about this.

What if you have got stuck on the other person's *No* somewhere? Then I suggest you write down the agreements you *have* got, and the point that the other *cannot* agree, then adjourn while you both think how to move forward.

It may be worth remembering that you're no worse off if the other cannot agree – just no better. You can still do whatever you think is right, and probably will. Just as the other will do what she or he thinks is right, too.

If you've got a problem-solving agreement

Firstly, you will both be feeling better about the situation because you have been able to agree some, if not all, things instead of continuing to disagree. Sometimes this alone seems to make the problem almost magically dissolve. If not, move on by discussing these questions:

❑ What will have to happen before we can both say that the practical problems have been solved?
— This gives a list of the results you both want
❑ What will have to be done to make these happen?
— This gives a list of the actions to be taken
❑ Who's going to do what, by when?
— This makes it all happen

Now turn these ideas into a personal reality by writing a plan for yourself. Who is the person you are going to talk with? About what subject? When? What will you do to make it easier for the person to cooperate? What will you say to show that you want to cooperate and not to beat the other person? How will you get agreement?

What I'm going to do is . . .

✎

_____

_____

_____

_____

THREE SETS OF BASIC FACE-TO-FACE COMMUNICATION SKILLS

❏ *Getting a hearing*
  — how to behave so that other people accept and respect you, listen to you and understand what you say
❏ *Getting the information you need*
  — how to listen so that you get to know what others know and can use this data to move forward
❏ *Getting a workable agreement*
  — how to get agreement to something you can all support so that everyone *does* move forward

The sections that follow address these issues in detail, and suggest practical solutions to the many problems.

BASIC SKILLS 1: GETTING YOURSELF HEARD AND UNDERSTOOD

You may have had the irritating experience of going into a shop where two assistants were chatting, and finding that you have suddenly become invisible. They pay you no attention, and you might as well not be there: bad for the blood pressure. This raises the question of what makes people decide whether you are important or not. Should I give you my attention? Or do you not matter much?

We make up our minds about someone else on the basis of three sets of clues:

❏ what the person says;
❏ how they speak (loud/soft, fluent/halting and so on);
❏ how they look to us – their body language.

How important do you feel each one is? When you make up your mind about somebody, how much does each of these influence you? Write down some notes about your view of the three sets of clues.

My view of the importance of what people say:

✎

_____

_____

_____

_____

_____

_____

My view of the importance of the way people speak:

✎

_____

_____

_____

_____

_____

_____

My view of the importance of people's body language:

✎

_____

_____

_____

_____

_____

How important is body language?

All the research (and there is a great deal of it) suggests that body language is the most important part of any face-to-face message. The exact values vary from situation to situation, but the range is somewhere between 50 per cent and 80 per cent. The non-verbal message is very rich and complex. It includes the expression on your face, how close you stand to me, what you are doing with your hands and feet, what you are wearing, whether you look me in the eye, how relaxed you seem . . . and so on.

The next most important clue is the tone and nature of your voice. Depending on circumstances, this carries around 15–30 per cent of the message – the one which people pick up, that is, which is not necessarily the one you're trying to send. Can any of you lie successfully to your partner? Probably not. But can he or she lie successfully to you? Well, you wouldn't necessarily know, would you?

So, if those two together account for between 65 per cent and 95 per cent of what people pick up, then it does not leave much for the effect of the words. If you think this is wrong, consider the person who says 'I'm listening' but goes on working with bowed head and does not look at you. What do you believe: the words or the body language?

Or remember the last time you were depressed and someone, picking this up from your body language, asked if you were all right. Did you, by any chance, say 'I'm fine, thanks'?

Learning about body language

There are two factors that really matter: is your body saying what you want it to? And, can you interpret other people's body language? It is doubtful whether you can learn these things from books, especially the first, though there are some amusing and interesting books around – try *Body Language* by Allan Pease, published by Sheldon Press.

Many of us are not very aware of our body language. This is especially true of men, who may not notice the signals that they and others are sending, and who may often miss out on quite important things. Like whether someone is being truthful; whether *they* believe *you*; does he really mean it when he says that's his last offer; are you annoying the big boss with your proposal or does he like it; does she fancy you; and other such important matters. The best answer is to join a group or workshop about how to analyse the often confusing signals of body language, and discover what signals you are sending yourself. For now, though, here are some things to try:

❑ Start paying some conscious attention to people's body language – a good way is to watch TV regularly for ten minutes with the sound off.
❑ Make some notes about the body language of people who are liked, respected and listened to:
  — how do they stand or sit?
  — what sort of expressions do they have?
  — what are their hands and feet doing?
  — what kind of eye contact do they have?
  — what other non-verbal behaviour have they?
  — more subtly, are they doing anything that contradicts the rest of their positive body language and may thus be damaging them?
❑ Begin to behave with the positive body language of the people you like and respect and other people will begin to see you differently.

A couple of paradoxes

The first paradox is that, in order to be heard you have to behave like the sort of person who *is* heard. More about what this means in Chapter 3.

The second paradox is that, in order to be heard you may first have to show that *you* can hear. In over 25 years of helping people deal with difficulties at work, the most common complaint I hear is 'But he/she doesn't listen to me!' I conclude that none of us listens very well and that *improving communication* really means *improving listening*.

BASIC SKILLS 2:
GETTING THE INFORMATION YOU NEED

Real communication can only happen when people listen actively to one another. You may be feeling that it's the *other* person who needs to learn how to listen; however, it is much easier to change what *you* do than what they do. Not easy, admittedly – just easier. If you can learn to listen better, you are likely to notice that the other person starts to listen better as well – an interesting demonstration of the old saying that 'You get back what you give'.

Conversely, if people think you don't listen then you will not get their cooperation, and you will both move further away from any prospect of a winning result. Also, you need to know what they know or you will have inadequate data, and may make poor choices because of not knowing enough. Sadly, we all have an idiot voice inside our heads shouting 'Me, me, me!' It is very hard to tune out this interference for five minutes to listen properly and avoid *the dialogue of the deaf*.

Finding out what you need to know

Two things influence other people to tell you what you need to know:

❑ Do they trust you and feel it is safe to relax and talk?
❑ Can you ask the right questions and hear the answers? (More about asking questions in a moment)

I am assuming that you *are* trustworthy, will not misuse what people tell you and do try to keep your promises. If I *can* trust you, then how much I relax and tell you depends on our rapport. This is mostly established through body language and not by what you say. Do you look as if you are interested in me, listening to me and friendly, neither hostile nor indifferent?

The body language of somebody listening to me and interested in what I say . . .

What listening looks like

You will have spotted the main characteristics:

❏ the listener keeps looking at the speaker (though not staring) although the speaker may look away;
❏ the listener's body is 'open' – especially, the arms are not folded and the hands are open and in sight;
❏ the listener is more likely to be smiling than frowning, with a pleasant and encouraging expression;
❏ the listener looks relaxed but alert, neither tense nor slouching.

A useful mnemonic is **SOLER**:

S stand or sit *Straight*, turn your face *Squarely* to the other and *Smile*
O have an *Open* body position – no crossed legs or folded arms
L *Lean* towards the other person slightly, never away from them
E maintain *Eye contact* (but do not stare) and make *Encouraging* noises
R *Relax* and be comfortable (but stay alert and avoid slouching or fiddling with something)

To summarise: if you want people to listen to you then you must first show them that you're listening – and body language is the key.

Is this making you uncomfortable?

I have often noticed that if people are not used to considering the non-verbal messages they are sending then they may feel uncomfortable and self-conscious when they start to be aware of their body language.

You might be concentrating so hard on getting the 'right' body language that you cannot hear a word people are saying. Or you may find yourself disputing whether it matters to fold your arms, since 'I always fold my arms when I'm sitting down'.

Some interesting things about body language

❏ It has no words or sentences – but it does send bits of information which combine into messages.
❏ Those messages, which are sometimes clear and sometimes fuzzy, are mostly about your feelings.
❏ People can learn to read those messages with a fair degree of accuracy.
❏ You cannot *not* have body language – you are sending messages non-verbally all the time. Especially when you're trying not to!
❏ Your preferred body positions and movements *do* say something about the kind of person you are.
❏ If your words say one thing and your body another then people will believe your body, not your words.
❏ You can change how you're feeling by consciously changing your body language.

No, really?

That last statement may sound so unlikely that we had better look at it more closely. Two factors are involved:

❑ Firstly, your feelings and your body language are very closely linked; the link works in both directions.
❑ Secondly, how you feel depends a lot on how you see yourself reflected in others, on how they see you.

For instance, if you are not confident about something and your shoulders are therefore down, your body is tense, you are looking down and not at people, and your arms are folded . . . then you can make yourself feel better by standing up straight, untensing your muscles, unfolding your arms and smiling pleasantly at people.

Secondly, if you do those things then the people around will see you as confident and relaxed. Their body language will begin to transmit that message to you and when you 'read' it you will start to believe it too.

You can take advantage of this if you:

❑ become aware of how you want to look – find a model in the people around you;
❑ become equally aware of how you look now and how that differs from your model;
❑ begin to behave as if you were the kind of person that you really want to be.

ASKING THE RIGHT QUESTIONS

So now you have started to arrange your body so that it sends useful messages to other people and gets them to listen to you and be ready to talk to you. You have also started to notice other people's non-verbal messages and begun to construe these. And you want to get the other person to talk so that two-way communication can begin between you. Now you actually have to get them to talk.

Good questioning skills are at the heart of good communication. As an old friend used to say, 'If you only know what you know then you have inadequate information'. Also, it is the person asking questions who controls the direction of the conversation. Which means, of course, that the junior or less powerful person can control a situation by asking the right questions. More about this in Chapter 3, when we look at situations in detail.

The essential difference is between the closed question, which gets a single fact, or a Yes/No answer; and the open question, which encourages the other person to talk. Most people know that, but still find it quite hard to think of good questions, so here are some suggestions.

Open questions get you started

❏ 'What happened when you went to see her?'
❏ 'How could we tackle this?'
❏ 'Tell me how you see the situation?'
❏ 'How do you feel about this?'

It is usually best to begin any encounter with open questions and narrow down to the details after you have got the overall picture.

Encouraging questions keep people going and explore issues

❏ 'Can you tell me a bit more about what you did?'
❏ 'And then what happened?'
❏ 'Go on, this is useful'
❏ 'How do you mean?'
❏ 'In what way?'

All these questions can restart people who have given you too short an answer first time round. Also, you can often keep people going by listening for key words in what they say and building these into your next question. If someone says 'Well, I had to put a stop to it'; your next question is 'So how did you set about putting a stop to it?'

Many people ask good first questions but never follow up properly, so they skate around on the surface and never get enough information.

Probing questions get depth and check accuracy

❏ "How did you reach that decision?"
❏ "What caused that, do you think?"
❏ "Tell me about the last time you noticed something like this."

Watch out for 'Why . . .?', as 'Why did you . . .?' and 'Why didn't you . . .?' feel like criticism or disapproval. Once you start to probe, it is important to keep your body language open and friendly, or you will begin to sound like the Gestapo and may meet resistance.

Closed questions get precise data

❏ 'What time was that?'
❏ 'Did you go?'

Also, you can turn 'How . . .?' into a closed question by adding certain words, as in 'How much . . .?' Closed questions are useful for checking details, but *not* good for getting either of you to relax and get rapport – they feel too inquisitorial. If the other person starts giving you short answers, or you feel stuck, try an open question to get things started again.

Questions to avoid

❏ *Leading questions* are not questions, but disguised state-ments. 'Don't you feel . . .?' really means 'I feel. . .', while 'Isn't it true that . . .?' is actually 'I think that . . .'.
❏ *Loaded questions* are not questions either, but expressions of disapproval. 'Can't you see that . . .?' and 'Don't you realise . . .?' both equal *'You twit!'* You are entitled to your views, of course; but pretending that they are questions is cheating!

Questions are only useful if you listen to the answers

Reflective responses back up your body language and signal that you really are listening. You focus on what seems to be the key issue and mirror it back. It is usually best to use statements, not questions: 'You feel . . .'; 'You think . . .'; 'You see this as . . .'. If you are not sure, preface your reflection with something that makes it tentative: 'It sounds as if you feel . . .'; 'I get the impression that . . .' to let the other person correct any misunderstandings. Also, if you reflect often you will find you won't need so many notes.

If you often summarise what both of you have said:

❑ things will become clearer to both of you;
❑ it will prove you were really listening;
❑ there will be a feeling of cooperation and agreement;
❑ you can close off a topic and start another.

If stuck for something to say, summarise what's been said.

BASIC SKILLS 3: GETTING AGREEMENT

The process of getting agreement draws together and summarises what we have been discussing here:

❑ Establish rapport, using useful non-verbal behaviour (pages 26–29);
❑ Set up a problem-solving agreement with the other person (pages 20–21);
❑ Focus on a joint solution (page 21);
❑ Ask questions to get the other person's views (pages 29–31);
❑ Behave positively so that you get a hearing for your views (pages 24–25);
❑ Look for what you can agree and summarise that (page 32);
❑ Repeat the process until the two of you have settled the main issues by agreeing action to deal with them;

❑ Write, together, an agreed statement of outcomes and actions, with schedules and deadlines;
❑ Go and do what you agreed.

In Chapter 3 we'll look in detail at how you can use the right style of communicating, while in the Checklists we'll make these principles work in particular cases.

SUMMARY

This chapter considered:

❑ getting cooperation and a problem-solving agreement;
❑ getting yourself heard and understood;
❑ making more use of non-verbal methods;
❑ finding out what you need to know;
❑ asking the right questions;
❑ reaching an agreement.

EXPERIMENTS

Getting cooperation from somebody

Who will you try the experiment of pages 20–21 with? Pick somebody who is not *very* hostile to start with so as not to load the dice too much; and pick something which is not a major bone of contention between you. You can always go for something harder later if this works.

Getting yourself heard and understood

Think of somebody that you, and others, respect and admire. What is that person's body language? How do they speak? What kind of things do they say? Which of these things will you try to learn so that people respect and admire you a bit more?

Making more use of non-verbal methods

Next time you are with somebody else, take a second or two to become aware of what your body is doing. What position is it in, where are you looking, what are your hands and feet doing? And, once you have tuned in to those, are they sending the same message as your words? Or are you saying one thing and doing another?

Finding out what you need to know

What extra information would be useful to you – at work, or not? Who knows this? Pick someone that you don 't get on very well with. Use pages 32–33 to plan how you will set up a meeting with this person and what questions you will ask. Don't try to *tell* the person anything, just concentrate very hard on finding out something you didn't know. And when you have, try summarising it accurately to the person before thanking them and going away.

3

FACE TO FACE

WHAT'S TRICKY FOR YOU?

This chapter builds on the last one. Here is a list of potentially tricky situations. How awkward each one is for you probably depends on who you are with, so you have to consider being with people senior to you, colleagues on the same level and people junior to you. Tick the situations you can handle well; put a cross against the ones you have not yet learnt how to handle well.

When I'm with my ...	Seniors	Colleagues	Juniors
Getting a busy person's attention			
Putting my point across			
Persuading someone to change			
Handling complaints from others			
Being praised or complimented			
Dealing with an angry person			
Dealing with an aggressive person			
Dealing with a very upset person			
Talking about my feelings			
Training or coaching someone			
Getting attention at a meeting			
Disagreeing with someone			
Criticising someone			
Praising someone			

When I'm with my ...	Seniors	Colleagues	Juniors
Getting honest and useful feedback			
Handling feedback positively			
Asking for something I want			
Refusing things I don't want to do			
Resolving a clash of priorities			
Broaching sensitive subjects			
Someone who talks too much			

WHAT CONCLUSIONS DO YOU DRAW?

Have a look back at your answers. The chances are that it seems harder to deal with senior people (or potentially awkward ones) than with others. Chapter 2 considered ways to get somebody else's cooperation, but there is another part to the equation: *how confident do you feel?*

This is where the other person's status and attitude can change your feelings quite drastically. You may be looking for someone's cooperation, but not be confident of your ability to keep your end up; or vice versa. And that, of course, affects how you will try to deal with any conflict or disagreement. Figure 3.1 shows the five possible styles for managing conflict and disagreement.

MORE ABOUT THE FIVE STYLES

'Go for it!' – when you feel confident but uncooperative

Some people maintain this style all the time. They crackle with aggression, believe in 'Ready! Fire! Aim!', and get into lots of arguments (many of them unnecessary) – Rab C Nesbit springs to mind. Some people only move into this style when they feel more powerful than the other person. Basil Fawlty was very good at this kind of bullying, but caved in fast if Sybil arrived.

Confidence

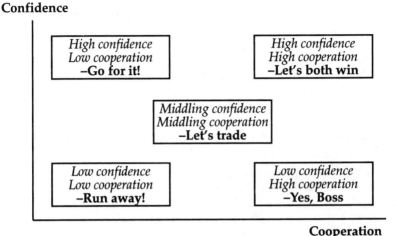

Figure 3.1 *Managing conflict and disagreement*

This style tends not to get other people's cooperation and may even make enemies, so it is a rather lonely and isolated approach which can produce a lot of emotional broken glass. 'I'm going to win, and I don't care who loses' is not very effective at solving problems. It also tends to push other people to either 'Run away!' or whimper 'Yes, Boss'.

'Run away!' – when you don't feel confident or cooperative

It is easy to be coerced into this style by someone aggressive or angry. You do not feel powerful enough to stand up to the other person, and you can't see why *you* should be the one to do all the cooperating when the other person doesn't do any. This leaves only avoiding the person – or, maybe, avoiding the issues. This is a very good way to collect lots of bad feelings – resentment, frustration, irritation at yourself for being so wet. These suppressed emotions may either fester inside you or burst out aggressively when you just can't bear it any longer.

'Yes, Boss' – when you feel cooperative but unconfident

Many people were brought up to be obedient, helpful and cooperative, to avoid upsetting others (especially superiors), to conceal negative feelings and try always to look calm. They may also feel that it's rude to ask directly for what they want, so they have to drop hints and hope people will guess right. This is a marvellous way to set yourself up for frustration, since most of us are not very good mind-readers.

Clearly, it's valuable to be cooperative, but you also need to be confident enough to put your point of view, ask for what you want and negotiate practical ways forward. You may also have noticed that you can't buy a relationship of mutual respect by always giving in – the other person just walks all over you.

People who use this style a lot may be doing it because they dislike aggression and conflict. The irony is that suppressing their own wants often builds up such a head of steam that they eventually become aggressive.

'Let's Trade' – when you feel partly cooperative and confident

This style actively seeks a practical compromise that both parties can live with, so has some advantages. It involves both giving up something they'd quite like in order to get something they really want, and stresses the importance of reaching a workable agreement. It is thus more likely to produce effective action than the three earlier styles. If both sides get something they want, then they may stick to the agreement and move forward.

People tend to aim for compromise when they want a practical result but don't fully trust the other person. They may thus not be fully open or direct, and they may try to manipulate, coerce or cheat the other person so as to win 'a bigger slice of the cake'. This usually has short-term gains and long-term severe losses.

Nevertheless, 'Let's Trade' can be a successful and practical style. Most people are open to negotiation, because it offers the possibility of gain and improvement. People used to saying 'Yes, Boss' all the time will find it reasonably easy to move to 'Let's Trade, Boss'.

'Let's Both Win' – mutual cooperation and confidence

The main difference between this and the other styles is that you concentrate on resolving the issues instead of trying to beat the other person (or defend yourself against a real or imagined threat). The two people work together to get the best possible answer for both of them. This sounds at first like compromise; but compromise assumes that 'the cake' has a finite size. If you feel it has, you also feel that if the other person has a bigger slice then you will have to settle for a smaller one. Back to defending yourself!

However, 'the cake' is often not finite at all, and two people who work together on the problems can usually create real benefits for one another. It means setting up a climate of mutual trust and cooperation, so the other person will have to trust you. That will only happen if you show (not say) that you're trustworthy.

HOW TO MAKE 'LET'S BOTH WIN' WORK FOR YOU

You will only be able to make this style work if:

❏   you want to benefit from the situation;
❏   you want the other person to benefit from the situation;
❏   you want to improve the relationship;
❏   you can behave in a trustworthy way;
❏   you can concentrate on solving differences practically;
❏   you can stop trying to score points or beat the other;

❏ you can consider the other person, plan what to do, work out what to say, and stay calm while you say it and negotiate a mutually-beneficial solution.

'Let's Both Win' is not easy to use, but it's the most promising style to start with, since it offers workable solutions – and no hard feelings either way. Also, if you begin with this style and it doesn't work, then you have the other four to fall back on. If you start with another style and that fails, then you won't have the right conditions for falling back on 'Let's Both Win'.

WHAT ARE YOUR PREFERENCES?

There are questionnaires which aim to diagnose your preferred style. However, as an intelligent person you know a bit about yourself, so I propose to ask you to decide for yourself.

First, identify five different disagreements you've had with somebody else:

❏ One where you're pleased with the result
❏ One where you're unhappy with the result
❏ One where you think the other person is still unhappy
❏ One where you think the other person is pleased
❏ One where you know you're *both* pleased.

Now think back to how you approached each of these situations and make some notes:

❏ Which style did you use to start with for each one?
❏ What other styles did you use?
❏ What style did you use *most* often?
❏ What style did you use *least* often?
❏ What style worked best?
❏ What style worked worst?

Record your conclusions here.

The conflict-management style I tend to use most is . . .

_____

_____

_____

_____

_____

The conflict-management style I tend to fall back on is . . .

✎
_____

_____

_____

_____

_____

The conflict-management style I tend to use least is . . .

✎
_____

_____

_____

_____

_____

The benefits of my preferences are . . .

✎
_____

_____

_____

_____

_____

_____

The drawbacks of my preferences are . . .

✎

_____

_____

_____

_____

_____

SUMMARY

Five styles of communicating to manage conflict:

❏ **'Go for it!'**, in which you win and the other person loses;
❏ **'Run away!'**, in which you both lose;
❏ **'Yes, Boss'**, in which you let the other person win;
❏ **'Let's Trade'**, in which you both win a bit (and lose a bit);
❏ **'Let's Both Win'**, in which you help one another to win as much as you both can.

EXPERIMENTS

What tricky ones will you tackle?

Go back to the choices you made on the form at the start of this chapter. To make a start, pick an easy one of those which you'd like to improve, and think of a real person you might be able to use as your guinea pig.

The situation I want to handle better is ...

✎
_____

_____

_____

_____

_____

On a 1–10 scale, I'd mark my ability at handling this situation as ...

✎
_____

_____

_____

_____

_____

What I'd have to be doing before I could mark myself one point higher. . .

✎
_____

_____

_____

_____

_____

_____

The communicating style that would suit this best . . .

✎

_____

_____

_____

_____

_____

The communicating style that I must avoid using for this . . .

✎

_____

_____

_____

_____

_____

What I'm now going to do about this (in detail, please!) . . .

✎

_____

_____

_____

_____

_____

_____

When you've had a go at this, reflect on what happened and make some notes here.

The style I actually used most was . . .

✎

_____

_____

_____

_____

_____

Good results from this . . .

✎

_____

_____

_____

_____

_____

Results I'd have liked but didn't get . . .

✎

_____

_____

_____

_____

_____

_____

Things to remember to do next time . . .

✎
_____

_____

_____

_____

_____

Things to remember to avoid next time . . .

✎
_____

_____

_____

_____

_____

Now see if you can improve your results, either with the same kind of situation or with another one from the form on pages 35–36.

The situation I want to handle better is . . .

✎
_____

_____

_____

_____

_____

_____

On a 1–10 scale, I'd mark my ability at handling this situation as . . .

✎
_____

_____

_____

_____

_____

_____

What I'd have to be doing before I could mark myself one point higher. . .

✎
_____

_____

_____

_____

_____

The communicating style that would suit this best . . .

The communicating style that I must avoid using for this . . .

What I'm now going to do about this (again, in detail) . . .

And when you've had another go, record what happened, on the form which follows. This approach of improving in easy stages gives you the best chances.

The style I actually used most was . . .

Good results from this . . .

Results I'd have liked but didn't get . . .

Things to remember to do next time . . .

Things to remember to avoid next time . . .

4

PLANNING AND PREPARING A TALK

MAIN CONCERNS

I have been helping people learn how to give talks since 1970 – somewhere between two and three hundred a year – so I have some idea of what might bother you about it:

❏ How do I control my nerves and build my confidence?
❏ How do I prepare and what do I put in and leave out?
❏ What kind of working notes will be best on the day?
❏ What are the useful things to do during the talk?
❏ How do I deal with questions from the audience?
❏ What about visual aids?

There are other things, of course, but once you can handle these (and yes, you *can*!) then the rest will come with practice, especially if you can get feedback on how you're doing in a supportive and helpful practice situation.

HOW TO PREPARE

To start with, what do you feel about giving a talk? Here are some simple ideas on the main issues involved in preparing and giving talks, arranged in ten sections. For each section, tick **two** (and only two) ideas that come close to what you feel.

1. You should start preparing a talk by ...

a writing down everything you want to say ☐

b jotting down a few ideas on paper ☐

c deciding what results you want to get ☐

d asking other people for some ideas ☐

e working off a talk given by the last person ☐

f deciding what your audience wants to get ☐

2. Nerves about giving a talk are something ...

a you can learn to handle positively ☐

b you shouldn't feel and should 'snap out of' ☐

c most people do not feel ☐

d even experienced speakers feel ☐

e you just have to live with ☐

f you will lose with experience. ☐

3. To speak for 20 minutes, you should allow about ...

a half an hour for preparation ☐

b an hour for preparation ☐

c two hours for preparation ☐

d four hours for preparation ☐

e six hours for preparation ☐

f eight hours for preparation. ☐

4. Your speaking notes should ...

a be typewritten for maximum clarity ☐

b be written extra large on small cards ☐

c contain every word you're going to say ☐

d be learnt off by heart ☐

e have key words for every main idea ☐

f only be a brief list of headings. ☐

5. *The most important things in a talk are to ...*

a get through it without hesitations ☐

b concentrate on saying what you know ☐

c get the audience involved ☐

d look everybody in the eye frequently ☐

e say exactly what you planned to say ☐

f stop questions from distracting you. ☐

6. *The visual aids will ...*

a contain as few words as possible ☐

b repeat most of the words you say ☐

c be designed as the last bit of preparation ☐

d be the main thing that people remember ☐

e be a complete summary of your talk ☐

f only work if professionally produced. ☐

7. *Questions from the audience are ...*

a likely to make you more relaxed ☐

b a distracting nuisance ☐

c probably intended to catch you out ☐

d a good way to get rapport with people ☐

e best at the end of the talk ☐

f a chance to show what you really know. ☐

8. People will probably remember ...

a most of your talk ☐

b about half of your talk ☐

c somewhere between a third and a half ☐

d about ten per cent ☐

e the beginning and the end ☐

f about half a dozen points. ☐

9. The best way to end a talk is to ...

a end with the action you want ☐

b ask for questions ☐

c get out quick before they ask questions ☐

d stop if you run out of things to say ☐

e summarise the main points ☐

f have someone else ready to take over. ☐

10. The best way to be persuasive is to ...

a present as many advantages as possible ☐

b make a very polished, watertight case ☐

c argue forcibly against any opposition ☐

d ask questions and summarise the answers ☐

e start with common ground ☐

f sell hard and discourage debate. ☐

I'll offer some comments on the ideas later, but for now jot down where you are as far as talks are concerned.

For talks and presentations, I can handle . . .

_____

_____

_____

_____

_____

_____

For talks and presentations, I haven't yet found out how to . . .

_____

_____

_____

_____

_____

_____

_____

HOW TO IMPROVE

Here are some comments on the ideas, based on 25 years of working with presenters in all sorts of situations; and some marks.

1. Starting to prepare a talk

a If you try to start without an objective then your notes will be unstructured – 0

b No objectives: 'If you do not know where you're going, you will end up somewhere else!' – 0

c Absolutely! Start by defining your objectives, then decide how to get them – 5

d Could be quite useful if you choose the people well – 2

e I think this is a lousy idea; it almost always makes trouble for the speaker – 0

f Very useful; try asking representative people what they know, and what they'd like – 5

2. Nervousness about giving a talk

a Yes, you may always be keyed up but you do not have to be gibbering – 5

b Ordering people to stop feeling something is not really helpful – 0

c Simply untrue; the ones who aren't nervous ought to be! – 0

d Quite true; all of us feel sharpened and apprehensive, but use this positively – 5

e No, I do not think you just have to put up with nervousness – 0

f Perhaps, but only if you get good feedback and can actually learn from it – 2

3. Preparation time for a 20 minute talk

a There's a very good chance you will feel unprepared and very nervous – 0

b Better, but still not nearly long enough – 0

c Better still, but you still haven't got time to organise yourself properly – 1

d You might just make some sort of shot at it – 2

e Most of us need about this amount of time to do a decent job – 5

f And some of us need this amount of time before we get it right – 5

4. Your speaking notes

a Popular fallacy, this; what will actually happen is that you will lose your place – *0*

b Extra large, so you can read them easily; small cards, so you can manage them easily – *5*

c You *will* lose your place; you will also be an Olympic-class bore – *0*

d This really is not necessary; learn beginning and end, maybe, but not the rest – *0*

e You're not inventing it as you go; key words remind you of what you decided to say – *5*

f If it is just brief headings, it may not remind you of what you want to say – *2*

5. The most important things in a talk

a Quite unreasonable – everybody hesitates when speaking naturally – *0*

b Dangerous; you always know more than you have got time to say, so may overrun – *2*

c Yes indeed! And there are lots of ways of achieving this essential result – *5*

d This is the one thing you can't do without – *5*

e Some merit in this, but it is usually best to have some flexibility – *2*

f BONNNGGGG! Real communication is two-way, not a monologue – *0*

6. The visual aids

a Quite so; words aren't visual. You need lots of images and pictures instead – *5*

b The most boring visual you have ever seen; what did it have on it? Yes, just words – *0*

c Visuals aren't an afterthought; they ought to be built in early – *0*

d Yes, this is very likely, since many people think in pictures – *5* e Some merit in this, but could be boring. Handouts would be better – *2*

f Not so; anybody can learn to produce effective visuals even if they can't draw – *0*

7. Questions from the audience

a I know this sounds odd, but it is true; try it and you will see – *5*

b They're only a nuisance if you really do not want to communicate effectively – *0*

c This is rarely true, but speakers who feel this behave aggressively and get problems – *0*

d Yes, probably the best way to get rapport and communicate persuasively – *5*

e No, it is best to build in intermediate question periods or let people interrupt – *2*

f No, they're a chance for the listeners to get answers to their questions – *0*

8. What people will probably remember

a You're going to be badly disappointed; memory just is not that good – *0*

b Still very unrealistic – *0*

c Well, maybe; but only if you have structured it very well indeed – *2*

d Pretty realistic; but will it be the ten per cent you want them to remember? – *4*

e Yes, very likely, as long as you're structured and do not ramble – *5*

f Again, very likely, so structure it to make those points really memorable – *5*

9. The best ways to end a talk

a Yes, an excellent idea, since people remember the end pretty well – *5*

b Better than nothing, I suppose – *2*

c BONNNGGG! – *0*

d This is a good way to make people remember you as a twit –
   0
e Oh good, you guessed it! – *5*
f This could actually damage your powerful final statement –
   0

10. The best ways to be persuasive

a Trying to cover too much delivers egg to the face; stick to a
   few major benefits – *0*
b Sometimes works, but people may be dissatisfied and may
   not actually agree – *2*
c Good way to start a fight and turn people off – *0*
   d Absolutely; construct a dialogue that takes account of
      everyone's views – *5*
e Yes again; get people to agree early on and they may keep on
   agreeing – *5*
f I fear this may end in tears – *0*

Jot down here how you might improve:

_____

_____

_____

_____

_____

_____

MANAGING YOUR NERVES

You can sabotage yourself – please don't!

First of all, what's your view of the audience at your talk? Do
you feel they're a group of critical and awkward people who:
❏ know far more than you do;

❑ are more powerful and strong than you;
❑ want to put you down;
❑ are just waiting for you to make a mistake

so that they can laugh at you?

It is easy to talk yourself into feeling like this, so that you want to run off and hide in a corner, whimpering. Easy, and quite wrong. Think, now: when *you* are in the audience, you think about the speaker 'I hope this person. . .

❑ is interesting;
❑ has prepared so it makes sense;
❑ gets me involved instead of talking at me;
❑ maybe even is witty

. . . and God forbid the person should make a mistake because that'd be so embarrassing for all of us'.

Please remember this: *The audience is on your side and wants you to do well!*

Some more ideas on managing your nerves

❑ Give yourself lots of time to prepare a talk – allow 25 times the talking time, so a five minute talk needs two hours preparation, and pro rata. *Do not* put it off till the day before; *do* get yourself properly organised and prepared – it'll make you feel less nervous.

❑ You're probably nervous – most of us are, even the professionals – but you can behave *as if* you're not nervous, and then we'll all believe it. Confident people stand up straight, with their heads up so they can (and often do) give everybody eye contact; their hands are open, their arms *aren't* folded, they *do not* fiddle with a pen; and their movements are slow and calm. You can do those things and you also will look confident.

❑ The swan floats on the millpond: calm, serene, majestic, beautiful, relaxed. It is actually paddling like hell, but only the swan knows that. After 25 years of discussing talks with people and watching them I'm absolutely convinced that you *do not* look as nervous as you feel. Remember this: it does not really show!

❑ Real conversation is not nearly so nervous-making as giving a talk. So try to get the audience to say something in the first five minutes; get a bit of dialogue going, because it will make you feel much better and much less lonely.

❑ If you feel really panicky in the few minutes before the start, sit down and concentrate on taking three or four really deep, slow breaths – it'll help.

PLANNING YOUR TALK

This section takes you step by step through the process of planning and preparing a good talk. Get a notepad and record your answers to the questions – it helps to number them, or write down the questions, so you can find your place.

1. What's your subject?

Sometimes this is given to you; even then you can usually decide *exactly* what it is you are going to talk about. Never try to do too much in one talk: a clear 20 minutes that makes sense, on one limited topic, is much better than a rambling hour that contains lots of information but feels fuzzy. Think about talks you have heard that really worked (always useful for any doubtful matter), and model your talk on them.

Decide the title of your talk (best if it is about five simple words) and write this down now.

2. Who are the people you will be talking to?

❑ **When you know the names of the people in the audience:** This often also means that you could, if you wanted to, talk to these people and get some idea of what they wanted and what they thought. Ring them up to find out what they know and what they want, and use this to focus your talk.

❑ **When you know what kind of people will be in the audience:** This means you have to do some guessing about their views when you plan your presentation, unless you can find and talk with some people who are like them.

Whichever case it is, write down now either the names of the people in your audience, or a description of the kind of people they are – 'the manager and most of the staff of the maintenance department' . . . 'a group of primary-school teachers' . . . 'people interested in child care' and so on.

3. What will people know after you have spoken?

Answering this question will give you half of your objective. What is it that you want people to take away from your talk? Jot down now the main things you'd like people to know about this topic. Keep it fairly simple at this stage.

4. What do you want people to do?

❑ **What do you want them to do during the talk?** Pay attention, obviously; but what else?
— Take notes, or will you give them a handout?
— Keep questions until the end? Ask questions at times you have pre-set during the talk? (better) Ask questions any time? (best, if you can handle this)
— Discuss things with you? Each other? In a group?
❑ — Anything else you want them to do (or *not* do?)

Decide what you want them to do for this talk and write it down now.

❑ **What do you want them to do at the end, or later?** This is your chance to check if you have got through. If you ask them to do something, and they do it, then the talk has been successful. If you chicken out of asking them clearly to do anything, then you may never know if it worked. Possibilities include asking them:
— to make a decision in your favour;
— to authorise you to take action;
— to take some action themselves;
— to do something positive about the topic.

Write down what you'd like them to do after the talk.

5. What do they know now, before you have spoken?

Answering this question will give you some idea of what level to start the talk at. You should assume that the audience are intelligent, but probably *do not* know much about the technicalities of your subject. If one of them does happen to be an expert, that person will usually *not* mind getting your fresh view of the subject, as long as you're organised, interesting and not talking down to people.

Jot down now some notes of what you think people know about your subject. Consider asking them.

6. What do they want from this talk?

There are some basics plus whatever is special for this audience this time. Basics:

❏ an interesting talk that gives them something useful;
❏ an organised structure, with some good visuals and perhaps some handouts;
❏ *not* a lot of technical detail, but some clear ideas that they can use themselves;
❏ to be involved in some way and *not* to be talked at;
❏ *not* to be talked at for much more than 25 minutes;
❏ a speaker who's not too nervous, does not get into difficulties, and does do well.

What else special does your audience want? What questions might they have beforehand? What could you give them that they'd appreciate?
Note – ring people up for ideas if you're not sure.

7. What's the common ground between you and them?

Now you know what you want to achieve *and* what they want to achieve. So, what is the common ground between you? Can you think of something you could say near the start which you think is true and they also think is true? Try to get everybody to nod and murmur agreement in the first minute – you will feel better and will move forward.

Write down your statement of common ground.

8. What are the essential sentences that people must understand and remember?

People usually cannot remember more than half-a-dozen points from a talk, even if it is a superb one. Do not expect too much of human nature! These main points are what you would really like people to remember. Visualise yourself two weeks after the talk asking people what they remember from it: what would you ideally like them to say? There will be a few major statements of what you and they want, expressed in simple language (no technical jargon), easy for any intelligent ordinary person to understand and usually less than twenty words.

'If we do not spend this money now we'll have to spend a lot more next year'.

'It is possible for you to learn how to do this, and you will enjoy it when you do'.

Decide your few main points and write them down. These would also make very good subjects for visual aids.

9. A sentence or so to introduce yourself

❑ your name (first name and surname is most natural);
❑ your job title, if anyone might not know you;
❑ a few words about what you spend most time doing;
❑ a word or two to say how long you have been dealing with the topic (it really does not matter how long that is – it is longer than they have been thinking about it!)

Good morning. I'm Pat Brooks, Materials Manager, and I spend most of my day seeing that people get the resources they need at the right time and in the right place. I have been designing a new inventory policy for a couple of months.

Now write down your one or two opening sentences.

10. A sentence on the benefit people will get from your talk

Pat Brooks might go on to say:

> By the end of this talk, you will know how to use the new system to get what you need when you need it, and I hope I'll have answered any worries you may have.

Write down what you will say so that people will know that your talk will give them what they want to know.

11. A sentence describing the common ground

Pat Brooks could get everybody on the same side with:

> We all want our systems to be easy and quick to use, effective in operation, cost-effective to run, and efficient at letting us all get on and do our jobs without hassle.

How will you express your statement of common ground to the audience? Work it out and write it down.

12. A short summary of your main points

Decide how you will summarise your main points at the end of the talk. If you want people to do something afterwards, then now's the time to say it clearly and specifically. People remember best the beginning and the end of a talk, so do not just trail off: end positively. Work this last bit out and write it down.

STRUCTURING YOUR TALK

Now you have got a completed plan of how you will start and finish, and a summary of the main points of your talk, focused on what you and the audience want. Now flesh out this skeleton with the right level of detail. Structure the talk to take account of the differences between levels of information (Figure 4.1).
Each of your main points will be clear if you:

❑ introduce the main point: *'Let's look now at the action we're suggesting'*;

❑ state it clearly: *'We recommend buying this widget'*;

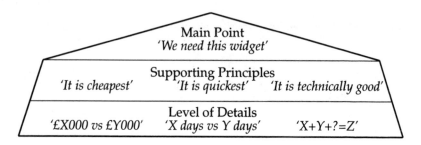

Figure 4.1 *Different levels of information*

❏ state the first supporting principle and its detailed proof: *'It is cheaper at £X000 than the rival widget at £Y000'*;
❏ do the same with the other supporting principles;
❏ restate the main point: *'So all of this means that the widget is our best answer'*;
❏ introduce the next main point : *'How, then, will we find the money to pay for it?'*

And so on. Do not worry about boring people by restating: it is a fact that people only hear about 20 per cent of what's said, so you *must* repeat your main points. But do not bang on about the details!

To decide what to keep in or leave out, classify information in the following order of priority:

❏ they *must* know this to understand and remember a main point;
❏ this would be useful in helping them understand and remember a main point;
❏ I like this and it would be nice for them to know (leave this out, please!);
❏ this is not really relevant to any of my main points (leave this out, too!).

VISUAL INTEREST

I know you haven't yet worked out exactly what you're going to say, but this is now a good time to pause and think about visual aids. Get those right, and you won't need so many notes for a start. People really do need something to look at, so do have some visuals – but make them *visual*, not just words.

Helpful visuals (especially if they have got colour in them) might include:

❑ some sort of plan at the start, to tell people what's going to happen – you might leave this up and tick off the main points as you cover them;
❑ pictures to illustrate, liven up and explain some or all of your main points – stick figures work well and so do icons, such as those used for public signs;
❑ a final picture that summarises your basic case or illustrates actions you want;

Avoid visuals which:

❑ are all words (especially if there are more than 10–15 words) and all in black text;
❑ have lettering that's too small or faint to read;
❑ have very complicated technical drawings, flow charts or diagrams;
❑ have too much detail (if you do not know what 'too much' is, ask your audience).

A way to make superb visuals is to find a computer near you that's running Microsoft Office and work through the tutorial on PowerPoint. It is very user-friendly, and you can get good results after half a day of learning. PowerPoint will also produce speaker's notes and audience handouts, so it is very versatile and well worth learning.

GETTING THE RIGHT WORKING NOTES

In the earlier sections, you have chosen the ideas you want to put across: at the *beginning*, to get started; in the *middle*, to make each of your main points clear and memorable; at the *end*, to summarise and finish well.

Now you need to produce the working notes that'll remind you of the next point to cover in the talk. Note: they *won't* tell you all the words to say; they *will* tell you what ideas to cover, and in what order. There are several reasons for this:

❑ If you had to read all the words off your notes then it'd be very boring, you couldn't make eye contact with people, and you might well lose your place.
❑ *Written* English is formal, rather stiff, full of long words and hard to understand when you hear it read.
❑ *Spoken* English is more informal and friendly, has simpler words, and is much easier to listen to and understand.

Compare the written version, 'An investigation was undertaken into X in order to determine . . .' with the spoken one, 'We investigated X to find out . . .'. The spoken one's shorter, too!

❑ If you write it all out and try to read that aloud, it'll take longer, be harder to understand and you'll seem more like a machine than a human.
❑ When you prepare, you plan what ideas to cover in what order; when you talk, you explain the ideas you have already worked out and thought through.
❑ This is *not* the same as ad-libbing but is using the notes to remind you of your plan.
❑ Finally, your working notes must be easy to read quickly and it must be *very* easy to find your place and see what's next.

This all means that your notes should be written **Extra Large** (perhaps printed in capital letters, with each point written on its own piece of paper. The notepads that come 10–11 cm square are good – and if you buy Oxfam ones you will get the bonus of a warm charitable glow!

There are two ways to produce this small stack of notes – commonly known as 'cribsheets' – each of which carries a reminder of one of your points. The longer way is to write out everything you plan to say, and you may want to do this if you're still not very sure. Then, <u>underline</u> all the <u>key words</u> in your <u>full version</u> of what you want to say and rewrite those on to your <u>final notes</u>.

The second way is to work straight from your plan, hooking out the ideas and writing those down as key words on your stack of note sheets. Once you have gained more confidence in this easier and faster method, you will probably start using it.

Choose your preferred method and write out your working notes now.

SUMMARY

❑ *Manage your nerves:* prepare well, behave as if you're not nervous, remember the swan, get a dialogue going, control your breathing (pages 59–61).

❑ *Define your audience:* talk to representative people in advance (pages 61–62).

❑ *Set your objectives:* what they will know and do after your talk (page 62).

❑ *Set their objectives:* what they know now, and what they want to know (page 63).

❑ *Find common ground:* get people to agree near the start (page 63).

❑ *Define the essentials:* the main points people must know (page 64).

❑ *Decide your introduction:* name, job title, what you do and how long you have been doing it; the benefit for the audience; common ground (pages 64–65).

❑ *Define final summary:* what you will say at the end of the talk (page 65).

❑ *Flesh out main points:* introduce each main point, state it clearly, expand, restate it (pages 65–66).

❑ *Plan your visuals:* pictures and not just words, colourful and interesting, large text and little of it, simplified and without detail, enhancing the main points of the talk (pages 66–67).

❑ *Get good notes:* spoken English, written BIG to be easy to read and navigate, triggers and reminders, written on small cards (pages 67–69).

EXPERIMENTS

Identify local opportunities for giving practice talks:

❑ Speaker's Club, where others will help?
❑ Parent-Teacher Association?
❑ Women's Institute or Church Institute?
❑ Your professional institute?
❑ Other local clubs and associations?

The idea is to find a forum where you could give a short talk about something that interests you to an audience which is not too critical or threatening. Most clubs and societies are very keen to find speakers, and you'd get useful practice.

5

DELIVERING A TALK

TRYING IT OUT

So now you have built on your planning form to get a set of good visuals and some usable notes, and it is all starting to feel more organised. Now you need to practise talking it through so as to smooth it out, adjust the details and get the timing right. No actor or musician would dream of going on stage without a rehearsal, so do it their way.

Rehearsals range from full-blown video'd ones in the actual presentation place with a skeleton audience, to just addressing your cat in the kitchen. However, they all have three things in common:

❏ you actually say the words out loud;
❏ you go through the motions of managing the visuals;
❏ you time yourself all the way through.

You have to speak out loud or the timing will be wrong (you read silently *much* faster than you can talk) and you have to practise managing the visuals or you may be clumsy and slow (for *how* to manage the visuals, see pages 73–76). And you have to time the talk because that's what the rehearsal is mostly for. If you can bear it, it is quite a good idea to audiotape yourself too. Whatever else you do, *do rehearse* – it always improves the talk.

MANAGING THE SETTING

You might be speaking anywhere from a draughty village hall to a fully-equipped lecture theatre, so *turn up half an hour early.*

Find out:

- ❏ what equipment you have got, which bits work, and where all the switches are;
- ❏ whether there's enough flip chart paper and pens that actually write;
- ❏ where you're going to stand or sit so that everybody can see and hear you;
- ❏ where you're going to put your notes and anything else you need.

For audiences of 25 people or fewer, it is best to put their chairs in a U-shape so that when you stand in the gap of the U everybody can see everybody else. *Never* use classroom-type layouts with adults, especially young adults – it gives the wrong feeling.

It is best *not* to use a public address system if you can possibly avoid it; they nearly always go wrong and alternate between squawks, whistles and silence!

MANAGING YOURSELF

Go back and reread pages 59–61, *Managing your nerves*, just to remind yourself of the main issues. Remember that you *can and will* cope with this – in an hour or so it'll be behind you. I assume you're apprehensive and keen to do well – there's something wrong if you *do not* feel keyed up, no matter how experienced you are. It is important to use this adrenaline rush to give you energy and dynamism, and to stop it pulling you off target or distracting you. Your body language is the key to getting this right.

Your body language reflects how you're feeling, so if you're feeling a bit threatened then that feeling may be 'leaking out' in what your body's doing. The 'swan effect' will be reducing what people see, but it'll be affecting you.

The link between feelings and body language works the other way round, too (see page 29), so if you deliberately make your body language positive and confident, then you'll start to feel more like that. Other people only know how you're feeling by what they see you do, so if they see you behaving positively and confidently then they'll believe it. And *their* non-verbal signs will reflect this, so they'll be sending you the message 'We think you're positive and confident'.

We're all nervous, but we can all behave as if we weren't. Key points:

❑ Move and speak slowly – it calms you and you'll look less tense.
❑ Stand or sit straight (but not tense) – do not lean.
❑ Keep facing people – do not turn your back on people to face screen or chart.
❑ Look everybody in the eye and smile at them a lot.
❑ Move if you need to be somewhere else – do not move about if you needn't.
❑ Keep your body 'open' – come out from behind the table or lectern, unfold your arms, uncross your legs, open your hands and keep them in view.
❑ If you get the dreaded 'shakes' (unlikely but possible) then sit down – or perch on the corner of a table.

Finally, if something goes wrong be ready to get the help of the listeners – they'll give it to you. Say something like 'Sorry – I have lost my place/dropped the next piece of paper/found this illegitimate projector does not work. Give me a minute to get sorted.' And they will.

MANAGING THE VISUAL AIDS

I hope you have got some – try pages 66 and 67 for advice on making them. For *all* the visual aids that you use, position yourself so that you keep looking at the listeners for nearly all the time – stand or sit *beside* your aids and not with them behind you. Also, practise on your own before using any aid.

Boards, black and white, and flip charts

❑ Plan to write only a little at a time – it takes longer than you expect. Just write bullet points and key words.
❑ Use these aids *mainly* to record what people say to you – this helps everybody.
❑ Remember to turn back and face the people after each time you write something – keep your toes pointing at them.
❑ Check that you aren't blocking somebody's view of what you have written.
❑ Write big, and try to keep your lines straight.
❑ Use a variety of colours to make it look more interesting.
❑ Consider drawing an outline in pencil ahead of the talk and filling it in as you go.
❑ If (like mine) your writing still looks untidy, then prepare transparencies instead (page 67 has some advice).

Overhead projectors

❑ It is best to sit beside the projector, facing the audience – do not block people's view.
❑ If you stand, remember to move to the side after using the projector.
❑ Keep facing the listeners – do not turn and look back at the screen, but keep pointing your toes at them.
❑ Make all the moves with the projector switched *off*, and make them *slowly*:
   — put the next transparency on the machine and line it up squarely
   — switch on
   — talk about what it says – but please *do not* boringly read it word-for-word
   — point out important bits with a pencil on top of the transparency
   — switch off
   — put the next transparency on the machine.

❑ Have a 'Ready' pile of transparencies and a 'Done' pile; keep the 'Done' pile in order so that you can refer back to them if necessary.

35 mm slide projectors

I know these are a good way to show photographs, but I do not like them, because:

❑ you have to put the lights out, so you won't be able to read your notes;
❑ projectors have moving parts and can go wrong in lots of creative ways;
❑ there are eight ways to put a slide in a carrier, but only one is right;
❑ when you drop a carrier, it will delay you for some time;
❑ if you have a projectionist to show your slides then you will have to rehearse with that person over and over (and over) again.

Having said that, if you want to use one then do – but remember:

❑ give yourself plenty of time to set up – it can take around 30 minutes;
❑ rehearse, rehearse and rehearse;
❑ have something to fall back on if the beastly thing goes crook on you.

Computer data projectors and LCD projection panels

A data projector is a self-contained unit that takes visuals (PowerPoint and the like) from a portable computer and shines them in glorious Technicolor on a screen. The images are sharp and clear and you can do lots of clever tricks. A projection panel does the same job (only not *quite* so well) but needs a separate overhead projector. The main snag is the cost – £4500 + for a projector, £2000 + for a projection panel, though they can be hired. Lovely pieces of kit, and *very* effective. If you have one, then (as the computer people say) *RTFM,* which stands for '*Read The Flaming Manual*' (or something similar).

Models, photographs and the like

These are an excellent idea, but:

❏ let people handle them if you can: pass them around or let people gather about you;
❏ when people are looking at things, *shut up* – do not distract them;
❏ use things like this to add interest and variety and give a break from you talking – good for you *and* the audience.

Handouts

Not visuals, strictly speaking, but they fall into the category of visual aids. Use them to provide details, to summarise *after* you have spoken and to break up the talk. Oh, and do shut up while people are reading them!

MANAGING QUESTIONS

You really need to get questions from the listeners, because then they stop being listeners and start to be fully involved. Presenters often worry about the question period, but it is likely to make you feel better, not worse. This is because it is more like an ordinary conversation, so usually feels more comfortable.

When can you have questions?

Questions near the start

Surprisingly, it is good to have a short question period near the start, because the dialogue will usually relax you, and will also help the listeners to feel more involved.
    You can nearly always ask people:

❑ *What's your experience of this topic?*
— A short discussion here can help you pitch at the right level of knowledge.
❑ *What would you like to know about it?*
— If you have prepared well, chances are you'll cover what they want to know, but asking them for details helps to involve and focus them.
— If somebody raises something you haven't prepared, say so and list it on a flip chart headed 'Unfinished business'. Then, at the end, ask people what they want you to do about the unfinished bits.

Questions at the very end

This very popular option:
❑ helps the presenter to keep control of time during the presentation;
❑ makes the listeners feel they're not really involved, as they cannot talk;
❑ means that people cannot have their questions answered when they want;
❑ is probably the *worst* option.

Questions all the way through

This option:
❑ is less common, because the presenter has to be able to control the discussion;
❑ makes the listeners relax and get properly involved;
❑ means people do not lose track because of having unanswered questions;
❑ is the best option, but try the next option if you do not feel quite ready to tackle questions all the way through yet.

Questions at several intermediate points

This very useful option:
❑ lets you break the talk up by building in questions after main points;

❏ keeps reasonable control of time;
❏ makes the listeners get reasonably involved;
❏ means people only have to wait a little time before getting an answer;
❏ is probably the best option for most people – a workable compromise.

ANSWERING QUESTIONS

It is important to:

❏ have a helpful and pleasant manner – do not be defensive!
❏ treat every question as a genuine request for information, *not* an attack;
❏ look at the questioner when she's speaking.

A useful standard procedure is:

❏ repeat the question if you want thinking time;
❏ answer it *briefly* – do not bang on, or raise extra points;
❏ check that the questioner's happy with the answer:
  — look at him, smile and raise an eyebrow, or ask 'OK?'
  — he'll nod if he's satisfied
  — if he does not nod, you haven't answered satisfactorily and must try again.

Never is quite a long time, but never, *never*, argue with your audience, or contradict them, patronise them, or put them down. If you do, you'll lose all credibility and might as well pack up and go home.

If you do not have an answer, try:

❏ 'I'll find out for you' – if you choose this, *do it*, do not duck it.
❏ 'This is an interesting one – what do people think?'
❏ 'I haven't come across this before – has anybody else?'
❏ 'It is a good question – what's your own view?'
❏ 'I think John knows more about this than I do.' (If you choose to pass the buck to an expert, or The Boss, give them a chance to refuse so that you do not put them in an embarrassing position.)

MANAGING THE AWKWARD 'SO AND SO'S'

Awkward people tend to come in two main flavours: the ones who want to tell everybody how much they know, and the ones who want to disagree with you. I have listened to thousands of talks (literally!) and the first sort are much more common than the second. The audience is usually neutral or on your side and will stay on your side if you involve them, treat them courteously, are organised and do not bang on too long. You might, however, get the odd individual who wants to have a go at you, so some ideas follow.

Managing people who want to tell you what they know

- ❏ *Never* argue or put them down, and do not get drawn off your point.
- ❏ They actually want to be helpful, so get them on your side.
- ❏ Wait till you can get a word in edgeways, then:
  - — do not respond to what they have said
  - — summarise what they have said, adding and subtracting nothing
  - — thank them and move on.

This maintains an atmosphere of friendly cooperation.

Managing those who disagree with you – some suggestions

- ❏ *Never* argue, contradict or put people down.
- ❏ *Always* summarise what they're saying before you respond:
  - — this gives you thinking time
  - — it also keeps tempers down and maintains friendly cooperation
  - — often people just want you to listen to their views.

❏ Try 'Yes, I can see that you might feel that' – refuse to get into a fight.

❏ Try to start your answers, 'Yes . . .' or 'Yes, and . . .' – *never* 'Yes, but . . .'.

❏ If contradicted on a detail, then accept this but restate the principle, 'Yes, some smokers do live a long time but the odds are against them.'

❏ If contradicted on a major principle, ask for facts; chances are the person is not as well prepared as you, but just does not like what you're saying. Try, 'I can see you feel strongly about this, but the facts contradict you'.

❏ Try asking the other people for their views.

❏ Try asking The Boss, or an expert, for their views.

❏ Try agreeing to differ, 'If I go on for the rest of the day, I suspect you won't be convinced. So do you think you'll change my mind?'

❏ If you absolutely *must* disagree, use 'Yes, some people would agree with you, but I'm with the majority who feel that . . .'.

❏ If you find you have got into a fight, stop immediately and arrange to discuss it with the person afterwards – you'll salvage a bit of credibility.

SUMMARY

This chapter considered delivering talks. Key points:

❏ Always rehearse your talk.
❏ Arrive half-an-hour early to set up.
❏ Expect to be nervous but expect to be able to handle this.
❏ Get your body language right so as to feel (and look) confident.
❏ Whatever visual aids you use, keep your toes pointing at the audience so that you keep facing them.
❏ Make all moves on an overhead projector with the machine switched *off*.

❑ Build in a question period near the start to relax you and the audience.
❑ Build in intermediate question periods to break up the talk.
❑ Be helpful and undefensive when answering questions, and keep your answers brief and to the point.
❑ *Never* argue, contradict or put people down.
❑ Use summaries to control discussions.

EXPERIMENT

I suggested on page 70 that you identify local opportunities for giving practice talks. If you did, well done – extend and repeat this so as to improve. However, you may have made some excuses to yourself for putting this off till a more convenient time.

Now's the time!

6

THE WRITING BUSINESS

SOME BASIC FACTORS

Face-to-face communication is not always easy, but it does let people work together towards agreement and action. Writing has some serious disadvantages:

- ❑ You cannot *see* (or hear) the reader's reactions and comments, so you cannot adjust what you say to make it more understandable or acceptable to an individual.
- ❑ It is hard to get the right 'tone of voice'.
- ❑ People who would pay attention to you face to face may ignore what you write.
- ❑ The whole process slows communication up.

Writing at work means coping with these limitations, and finding ways to get your readers to *want* to read you. And that means thinking hard about what people really want. Give your readers what they want and they may reciprocate; bore, annoy or confuse them and they are unlikely to help you.

THE ESSENTIAL PLANNING QUESTIONS

How can I start where the reader is to get early agreement?

- ❑ Who is your primary reader (or readers) – the people who will read for action?
  (*Who can say 'No' to what you are putting forward?*)

❑ What will your primary reader do with this document you are writing?
(*What does she need to get from you?*)
❑ Who are your secondary readers – the people who will read for information?
(What's the *minimum* that will stop them being upset?)

Where do I want to be?

❑ What are the results that this document has to get?
— what do you want people to know after reading it?
— what do you want people to do after reading it?

If you are not clear about these results then others *cannot* give them to you.

What structure will I have?

❑ What's the common ground between what your readers want and what you want? What statement can you start with that you both believe is true?
❑ What topics are suggested by the notes you've made so far?
— jot down some headings covering your main points
— write each heading on a Post-it™ sticky note.
❑ What's the right order for those topics?
— move the stickies around until you have a logical start, middle and end
— *or* use an outliner on your word processor to get the same results.

How will I summarise my case?

❑ Take each topic heading and write one sentence that summarises the point you want to make about it.
❑ If the heading is 'How will I summarise my case?' then the *Topic Sentence* would be 'Take each topic heading and write

one sentence that summarises the point you want to make about it.'
❏ The Topic Sentence is:
— a summary of your main point
— written as clearly as you can, with no jargon or long words
— no more than 25 words long.

Now put all your Topic Sentences together, in the same order as your stickies, and see if they give you an adequate summary of your document. You may find that the order now is not quite right, or that you have to put in an extra Topic Sentence (and heading) just to make the logic flow properly.

The really interesting thing about this approach is that now you've written the Summary before the document. Given how hard summaries are to write, this is pretty good going!

How do I prove my case?

❏ Take each Topic Sentence in turn. What extra detail will you need to add?
— what will make it easy for this reader to understand this Topic Sentence?
— what will make it easy for this reader to believe this Topic Sentence?
— what will make it easy for this reader to want to do what I ask?

Do not get seduced into adding lots of the detail that you find interesting unless you are absolutely sure that the reader shares your interest. Concentrate on offering two or three good reasons why people will get what they want if they do what you want.

Add the *minimum* that will prove or demonstrate your point, or draw the necessary conclusion. Never pad documents out – we are all pushed for time. Mark Twain commented 'I never write "metropolis" if I'll get paid the same for "city"', which seems eminently sensible.

One word of caution. Most people recognise very quickly when you are insincere, or over-selling, or trying to con them. Treat them as intelligent people who are busy, and motivated by intelligent self-interest, and do not push too hard.

How will I put it all together?

Now you have an initial Summary, a logical flow of topic headings, a Topic Sentence for each paragraph and the right amount of detail to add to each paragraph. Write the paragraphs containing that detail for each of the Topic Sentences. That gives you the bulk of the finished document.

You also need to write a good, clear title so that people can:

❑ identify quickly what class of documents this belongs to
❑ identify quickly what this particular document is about.

Now put the document aside for a bit: at least an hour and preferably a day or two.

THE ESSENTIAL REVISION QUESTIONS

Does it pass the basic checks?

When you come back to your document after a day or two, it should look and feel a bit different; does it still say what you meant? If you do not pick up a few corrections then you probably haven't left it alone for long enough.

How short can you make it?

Now try to shorten it, while still keeping the essential message intact. Editing hard improves all writing. Whoever it was who wrote: 'I am sorry this is such a long letter – I did not have time to write you a shorter one' had the right idea.

How easy is it to understand?

Try a *Fog Factor* analysis. Begin by counting out a hundred-word sample. What's the average sentence length within that sample?

For ordinary, everyday communication it should not be much more than 20 words. That *does not* mean every sentence should be 20 words long, but it does mean that you should not have *any* sentence that's close to 40 words long. If you often write long sentences then people will stop reading you. Call the average sentence length *Factor A*.

How many long words have you got in your 100 word sample? Take a 'long word' to be three syllables or more. I'd have to count 'av-er-age' and 'syll-a-ble' in this paragraph (*and* 'par-a-graph'!) Call this number *Factor B*. Add *Factor A* to *Factor B*; the total should not be much more than 25 if you want to be clear in your business writing.

(For this section, *Factor A* is 13 and *Factor B* is 7, totalling 20.)

Can readers find out what they want easily?

❑ How will your reader identify what this document is and what file it belongs to?
❑ How easy is it to see who the document came from?
❑ How will your reader find out what it is about?
❑ If there's more than one subject, are they split into paragraphs?
❑ If there are more than three subjects, do the paragraphs have headings?
❑ Can your reader easily summarise your points in his mind?
❑ Can your reader see clearly what you are asking her to do?
❑ What will your readers get if they do what you want?
❑ What will it cost them to do what you want?
❑ How likely are they to do what you want?

How can I make sure I pick up all the mistakes?

The short answer is that you'll usually notice the final mistake just as the MD is reading his copy. However, you can improve the odds a lot by making an agreement with a friendly colleague to proof-read one another's documents. This is because you'll read what you meant (and not what you actually wrote!) so you need someone else to see the typos, the bits of shaky logic, the technical gaps and the straight stupidities. Don't worry – nobody gets it right first time.

GRAMMAR AND PUNCTUATION

I've noticed that people are sometimes uneasy about their ability to write grammatically and to punctuate correctly. Some teaching methods do not suit some of us, and school may be a distant memory. You may also feel daunted by the prospect of restudying a boring and often incomprehensible subject. If this feels familiar, take heart – you *can* understand it!

This next section is based on the work of Ray Bailey, who deconfused the whole topic in a splendid book called *A Survival Kit for Writing English* (Bailey, R F, 1976, Longman). On the other hand, if grammar and punctuation hold no terrors for you then skip the next section (and feel smug).

The basics

Grammar and punctuation are mostly about being clear. 'Let's eat, Harry', is not the same as 'Let's eat Harry', especially for Harry. Good business English has a clear structure, is easy to read and understand, does not have any jargon or difficult words, and does not ramble.

Some simple rules

❑ A Control Unit can be a valid sentence on its own (*that is*).
❑ A Support Unit cannot be a sentence on its own (*so must be attached to a Control Unit*).
❑ Always punctuate between any two units, but not in the middle of a unit (*that's why the comma is where it is*).
❑ Control Units and Support Units are usually separated by commas, no matter which kind of unit comes first. No

Table 6.1 *Sentence construction*

A valid English sentence must have ...		and may also have ...	
a subject	*and a verb*	*an object*	
ie, a doer	what it is doing	ie,	a done-to
Like 'Jim	swore'	Like,	'at me'
	These two parts together are **a Minimum Control Unit**		

These three parts together are **a Full Control Unit**

Anything that does not have either a subject or a verb is **a Support Unit**

matter which kind of unit comes first, Control Units and Support Units are usually separated by commas. (*Both versions are correctly punctuated.*)

A few more rules

❏ Never separate Control Units with a comma, it is wrong to do this. (*There are two Control Units in this sentence, so the comma between them is wrong.*)
❏ Full stops are safe Control Unit separators. (*The last example could be corrected by making it 'Never separate Control Units with a comma. It is wrong to do this.'*)
❏ Full stops are safe Control Unit separators; semi-colons can also be used. (*The semi-colon in this example separates two Control Units.*)
❏ A colon signals an announcement: it is usually followed by a result, an explanation or a list. (*The colon here is followed by both an explanation and a list.*)
❏ Parentheses, *and this is one*, need pairs of separators.
❏ Parentheses – *and this is one* – need pairs of separators.
Parentheses (*and this is one*) need pairs of separators. (*All three possible pairs of separators are included in these examples.*)

❑ A string of adjectives needs special, clarifying, extra dividing commas between all the adjectives *except* the last two (*just like this example*).
❑ *Comma FANBOYS* reminds you which words usually have a comma in front of them:
,for ,and ,nor ,but ,or ,yet ,so.
❑ 'And' and 'but' only have a comma in front of them if they are starting a Support Unit.
❑ The dash ' – ' is best used sparingly in business writing. It usually suggests 'I'm working this out as I go along, and do not have much idea of what really matters'.

A good sentence in Business English . . .

❑ averages 20 words long; is never more than 40 words;
❑ must have a subject and a verb, and may have an object;
❑ is *one* idea, expressed as simply as possible.

A good paragraph in Business English . . .

❑ is *one* concept, expressed in a logical flow of simple ideas;
❑ has a clear label (*a heading or title*) for the concept;
❑ often ends with a conclusion or deduction;
❑ has a Fog Factor of less than 25.

To be sure of being clear and grammatically correct, KISS

❑ *K*eep *I*t *S*hort and *S*imple!

THE STRUCTURE OF BUSINESS REPORTS

Begin at the end

As Chapter 1 suggested, a good place to begin anything is with its purpose. In business reports, that means beginning by answering very briefly the questions 'Why was this report written? What's the point?'. Some possible ways to answer:

❏ State the brief or Terms of Reference.
❏ Describe the results the report is meant to achieve.
❏ Specify the work that has been done, and why.

Begin with the end

It helps to begin with a summary. This is because an intelligent reader will stop when she has got enough. Very senior people need only a summary. They are likely to get justifiably irritated if you make it hard for them to find out what they need to know.

The summary briefly sets out:

❏ where you started
❏ what you did
❏ what results you got
❏ what conclusions you reached
❏ what you recommend (if you were asked to recommend).

There has been much research into how easy a scientific or technical report is to read and understand. All researchers agree on the most important factor. What's your view?

The most important factor for readability and understandability is . . .

_____

_____

_____

_____

_____

_____

What makes something easy to read and understand?

Common sense suggests that the reader's familiarity with the topic might be the most important factor. In fact, though this obviously makes a difference, the structure of the report is far more important. An educated reader will *not* be able to understand a badly-structured report; a reader who is new to the topic *will* be able to understand a well-structured document. All the research shows that, of structural factors, the most influential is whether there is a summary or not.

A poor or non-existent summary means that all levels of reader take longer to understand and process the report. Give a good summary, and all readers read, learn and act on the report faster and more accurately.

The body of the report

There are many possible report structures, and the type of report usually dictates which is best. Suggestions:

❑ Past (what has happened); Present (what is happening); Future (what we want to happen)
❑ The present situation; the desired situation; possible ways to create it; the preferred way
❑ Objectives; opportunities for change; pros and cons of each; conclusion and recommendation
❑ Purpose; Summary; Actions; Results; Conclusions; Recommendations
❑ 5W-H (*What? Where? When? Who? Why? How?*). This is also a good way to check coverage of topics.

Principles in the Body, detail in the Appendix

The body of the text contains your message; the supporting details belong in an Appendix. They are then available for checking if needed, but not cluttering up the flow of your argument. Readers (like the Court) are mainly interested in your

verdict, and will only study the evidence if that verdict seems
odd or unjustified.

If you find that you are repeating a lot of details in either the
Summary or the body of the report then it suggests that your
structure has gone fuzzy. You may need to rethink.

Recommendations

Make sure that you fulfil the objective. If you were asked 'Is it
safe?', say either that it is or recommend how it could become
so. Also, does your evidence support your recommendations
fully? Many a report writer has made a wild stab of 'It must
therefore be true that . . .' when the branch that was doing the
supporting was already sawn through.

The key elements

❑ Plan from a clear structure to help yourself and your
  readers
❑ Write as plainly and briefly as you can:
  — prefer short words to long ones
  — prefer everyday words to jargon
  — prefer the short to the padded
  — prefer the plain to the fancy
  — prefer the facts to the opinions
  — prefer the natural to the formal.

DEALING WITH OTHER PEOPLE'S WRITING

Many of us have too much to read, and some of it is neither
interesting nor well written. This section offers some effective
ways to deal with what other people send you.

It helps to be able to read quickly and, while some people do
this naturally, anyone can learn to read faster *and* understand
more. You cannot learn the physical techniques of effective
reading from a book. However, if you are interested then find
out whether anyone teaches reading techniques in your area. It

is possible to double your reading speed while also increasing your comprehension and recall.

The techniques suggested here will *not* increase your reading speed, but they will:

❑ help you to understand and learn more of what you read;
❑ make it easier for you to remember important information;
❑ allow you to handle your paperwork faster.

They are based on what we know about how people learn best. You are constantly bombarded by information from all your senses, so what you read can easily be drowned out by 'noise'. To learn something new from a document, you have to make space for it in your busy mind. This means finding out where the new information will fit, since we learn best by making connections between what we know and what we want to know. It is as if the new data was a piece of a jigsaw puzzle which needs to be fitted into the right slot. This phenomenon is usually called *Mental Set*.

A complication is that you may not be receptive to anything new. It is hard to learn anything if you are tired, distracted, ill, bored ... and some documents are pretty good at boring or tiring you.

However, you can improve your learning by gaining an overview first and then adding more and more detail to it. This is because you need to grasp *the overall picture* before you can understand details. You must know what the jigsaw represents before you can fit in the separate pieces.

Also, you can fix information more firmly in your memory if you practise recalling and reviewing it. This not only improves your memory, it also tells you what parts you have not yet learnt fully, and so must re-read.

It helps to have several different ways of reading:

❑ *close study,* for understanding and remembering all of a vital document which is central to your work;
❑ *analysis,* for discovering exactly what you need to know from a long document or one that is not vital for you;
❑ *overview,* for getting a general understanding of some background or peripheral document.

This also suggests that you could deal more efficiently with your crowded in-tray by spending a moment or two categorising papers. Many of us use the following simple process.

Categorising your in-tray

❏ Identify each document from its title or reference.
❏ *Do not* read further yet, but put it in one of four piles:
— *Vital*, to be read first and with great attention
— *Useful*, to be analysed for valuable information soon
— *Background*, to be skimmed later for an overview
— *Ditch*, which you delegate, pass on or bin now.
❏ Go back to the *Vital* pile and deal with it.
❏ Get on with the rest of your work.
❏ Come back to the *Useful* and *Background* piles later.

THE THREE READING METHODS

Each method has the same structure:
❏ Prepare to understand the new information
❏ Find the new information in the document
❏ Acquire it as quickly as possible
❏ Consolidate it in your mind.

Close study reading

❏ Identify the document from its title or reference.
❏ Pause before you read, and ask yourself these questions:
— What do I know about this topic?
— What stage are we at?
— What do I expect this document to say?
— What do I need from this document?

(You may note down your answers, or just think them through in your head).
❏ Read the summary, if there is one.
❏ If there is no summary then read the first paragraph (to find out where the writer starts) and the last paragraph (to find out where the writer winds up).

❑ Review what you have learnt at this point – note it down.
  — Do you agree with the main points, or must you study the detailed evidence?
  — Have you discovered what you need to know? If so, do you *really* need to read any more?
❑ If there are headings and subheadings, scan the document quickly, reading *only* those.
  — Where is the information that you need to know? Go to it and study it in detail, making notes.
  — Which other parts do you need to read in detail?
  — Which parts do you need to scan for a broad picture?
❑ If there are *no* headings, try reading just the *first* sentence of every paragraph – it might be a summarising Topic Sentence (see pages 84–85). If so:
  — Where is the information that you need to know? Go to it and study it in detail, making notes.
  — Which other parts do you need to read in detail?
  — Which parts do you need to scan for a broad picture?
❑ Review what you have now learnt:
  — Have you discovered what you need to know?
  — What else have you discovered?
  — What new questions do you now have?
  — Where might those be answered?
❑ Re-read anything which you need to fix firmly in your mind.
❑ Consolidate by asking yourself these questions:
  — Now what do I know about this topic?
  — What conclusions do I draw from that?
  — What do I need to record?
  — What will I do?
❑ Make notes and take the appropriate action.

Analytical reading

❑ Identify the document from its title or reference.
❑ Pause before you read, and ask yourself these questions:
  — What do I know about this topic?

— What do I expect this document to say?
— What do I need from this document?
❏ Read the summary, if there is one.
❏ If there is no summary then read the first and last paragraphs.
❏ Review what you have learnt at this point.
❏ Have you discovered what you need to know? If so, do you *really* need to read any more?
❏ If there are headings and subheadings, scan the document quickly, reading *only* those. Or try reading just the *first* sentence of every paragraph:
— Where is the information that you need to know?
— Go to it and study it in detail, making notes.
— Do you need to read anything else?
❏ Review what you have now learnt.
— Have you discovered what you need to know?
— What else have you discovered?
— What new questions do you now have?
— Where might those be answered?
❏ Re-read anything which you need to fix firmly in your mind.
❏ Consolidate by asking yourself these questions:
— Now what do I know about this topic?
— What conclusions do I draw from that?
— What do I need to record?
— What will I do?
❏ Make notes and take the appropriate action.

Background reading

❏ Identify the document from its title or reference.
❏ Pause before you read, and ask yourself the questions:
— What do I know about this topic?
— What do I expect this document to say?
— Is there anything specific that I need from this?
❏ Read the summary, if there is one. If there is no summary then read the first and last paragraphs.

❏ Review what you have learnt at this point.
  — What do you now know about this topic?
  — Is that enough, and can you now do something else?
  — If you haven't got quite enough, try scanning the headings, or the first sentence of every paragraph.

Finally . . .

Please do not feel guilty about making a conscious decision to stop reading something that is no longer useful to you. I just hope it hasn't happened with this book!

SUMMARY

❏ Plan a good structure for your document:
  — Get common ground with your readers (pages 83–84)
  — Identify topics and write Topic Sentences (pages 84–85)
  — Add only the detail that you need (pages 85–86).

❏ Revise thoroughly:
  — Edit hard to make it brief (page 86)
  — Apply a Fog Factor analysis (pages 86–87)
  — Review the structure (page 87)
  — Proof-read (pages 87–88).

❏ Brush up on grammar and punctuation (pages 89–90).

❏ Structure your business reports:
  — Begin at the end – the purpose (page 90)
  — Begin *with* the end – a summary (page 91)
  — Choose a useful structure (page 92)
  — Put details in the appendix (page 92)
  — Get your recommendations right (page 93)
  — Key elements of reports (page 93).

❏ Dealing with other people's writing:
  — Learning from written information (pages 93–94)
  — Varying how you read (pages 94–95)
  — Categorising your in-tray (page 95).

EXPERIMENTS

I considered various experiments that you might try, but they all came down to the same suggestion in the end: *Experiment with the advice in this chapter on real situations.*

So I'm just going to leave it at that.

7

CHECKLISTS FOR DIFFICULT SITUATIONS

This chapter consists of checklists for managing some situations when communicating is especially difficult. I began with a long list of difficult situations and it became clear that this chapter could easily grow to overwhelm the book if everything were included. The chapter thus concentrates on six important situations which many people experience:

1. Selecting the right person for a job
2. Being selected for a job
3. Giving effective feedback to someone else
4. Coping with feedback from someone else
5. Running a meeting
6. Contributing effectively to a meeting.

Each checklist covers: *Objectives; Preparing; Getting Started; Main Do's and Don'ts; Ending Effectively; Afterwards.*

1: SELECTING THE RIGHT PERSON FOR A JOB

Objectives

- ❏ Choose the person who will:
  - — be good at doing the job
  - — give commitment and cooperation
  - — fit in well with other people
  - — need the minimum of training
  - — stay as long as you want
- ❏ Avoid breaking the law
- ❏ Create a good impression of your organisation.

Preparing

Analyse the job (*Tip: be realistic*):

- ❏ What are the key tasks?
- ❏ What standards must they be done to?
- ❏ What qualifications do others doing this job have?

From this, define the kind of person you want:

- ❏ What must the person be able to do at the start?
- ❏ What must the person be able to learn to do?
- ❏ What kinds of experience build these abilities?
  (*Tip: be flexible, not rigid*)
- ❏ What minimum qualifications are needed?
  (*Tip: don't set an unrealistically high level*)

Write a detailed specification:

- ❏ What *must* the person be? This provides your first coarse filter.
  (*Tip: concentrate on a few essentials*)
- ❏ What would the *ideal* person be? This helps to differentiate candidates.

Plan the interview:

- ❏ What topics will you cover, in what order?
- ❏ What questions will you ask?

❑ What information will you give people?
   (*Tip: details are best given in writing*)
❑ How will you ensure privacy?
❑ What other arrangements do you need to make?
❑ How will you ensure you are (and look) organised?

Check the legal requirements and your organisation's rules.

Getting started

❑ Remember 'There are two frightened people here' (Freud).
❑ Be friendly and human, but businesslike.
❑ Make your body language SOLER (page 27).
❑ Introduce yourself; share the aims and plan of the interview.
❑ Don't talk too much at the start.
❑ Ask easy questions to relax the candidate.
❑ Also ask 'Is there anything you'd like from me first?'

Ending effectively

❑ Summarise everything that's been said.
❑ Ask 'What have I *not* asked that you'd like to tell me?'
❑ Ask what questions the person has for you.
❑ Say what happens next and when you'll announce results.
❑ Thank the candidate.

Afterwards

❑ Compare all the candidates.
   — Which ones pass your *must* criteria?
   — Of those, which is closest to the ideal?
   — Check this person meets all your objectives
❑ Notify successful and unsuccessful candidates.
❑ Complete the paperwork.
❑ Review the process:
   — What worked well, and not so well?
   — What will you do, and *not* do, next time?

Table 7.1 *Main do's and don'ts*

Do	Don't
work to a plan and share this with the candidate	be disorganised or unnecessarily secretive
postpone judgement until you've collected all the data	make snap judgements on appearance or early answers
concentrate on exploring what people have done and how they've done it – it's the best guide to what they *will* do	ask 'How would you tackle . . .?' – it won't tell you very much and a clever candidate may be able to manipulate you
ask for specifics, as in 'Tell me about what happened the last time you . . .' – and follow these up in detail	ask general or superficial questions like 'How do you get on with people at work?'
help the candidate to do as well as possible	keep nit-picking for reasons to reject people
make sure the candidate does 75 per cent of the talking	monopolise the interview
use effective questions and summaries (pages 29–32)	ramble or waste time
keep summarising to improve clarity and memory	keep writing lots of notes – this destroys rapport
ask for contrary evidence. If the candidate looks good, ask 'What gives you difficulty?' Few of us are good at *everything*. And if the candidate looks bad, ask 'What are you good at?' and help people to overcome their natural modesty.	simplify and think that a good talker must also be a good worker, or that a silent candidate must be ineffective.
talk less than the other person	monopolise the conversation

2: BEING SELECTED FOR A JOB

Objectives

❑ Set up a good rapport with the interviewer.
❑ Present yourself positively:
  — control your nervousness
  — answer questions effectively
  — give the interviewer a spread of factual evidence.
❑ Discover enough about the job to decide if you want it.
❑ Avoid getting trapped in an unsuitable job.

Preparing

Analyse the job advertisement and any other papers you have:

❑ What will the successful applicant do in the job? What have you done that is similar?
❑ What skills do they specify? What have you done that uses those skills?
❑ What qualifications do they specify? Which ones do you have?
❑ What personal qualities do they specify? What have you done that uses those?

Find out as much as you can about the organisation, using libraries and reference books.

❑ What does the organisation do?
❑ What is special about it?
❑ Has it been in the news recently?
❑ Why is it recruiting for this post?

If you can find out the name of the recruiter, *or* if an agency is handling the process, phone the person and say something like, 'I don't want to waste your time by making a pointless application. What exactly are you looking for? What's the most important thing about the person you'll choose?'
Base your preparation on the preceding steps and consider:

❏ What will be the most important areas of interest to the interviewer?

❏ What specific questions are likely?

❏ Which of your specific experiences are relevant? Get ready to give details of specific events so that you can prove what you have done, and can do.

❏ Make up a kit of documents to support your application.

❏ How will you get there with 15 minutes to spare?

Prepare an answer to the question 'Tell me about yourself', which covers:

❏ your particular skills

❏ an achievement that demonstrates those skills

❏ your priorities and objectives at work.

Prepare an answer to the question 'Why should we hire you and not the next person?' which covers:

❏ something positive that makes you different from other people

❏ a success that you've had, perhaps when you had to compete with others in some way.

Prepare an answer to the question, 'Why are you applying to us?' which covers:

❏ what makes them different from their competitors

❏ some success they've had.

Prepare an answer to the question, 'Where do you see yourself in five years' time?' which covers:

❏ the progress you hope to make

❏ the things you hope to learn.

If a fact is against you, prepare an answer which stresses the *positive* aspects.

❏ If you made a mistake then talk about what you've learned from the experience.

❏ If you did something badly then talk about how you now do it differently.

❑ If you had a conflict with someone, talk about how you can now see the other's point of view, and how you now avoid getting into similar conflicts.

Getting started

❑ Make sure your body language is positive from the start:
  — review pages 27–29, especially SOLER on page 27
  — especially, maintain eye contact with the interviewer.
❑ Follow the interviewer's lead in where to sit, what topics to cover and so on.
❑ Expect to be asked easier questions near the beginning.
❑ If you feel panicky, try:
  — breathing deeply and slowly for a moment
  — listening carefully to the interviewer's questions
  — asking for the question to be repeated to give yourself time.

Ending effectively

If asked 'What do you want to ask?', consider:

❑ 'What's the most important thing you want for this particular job?'
❑ 'How do you see the job developing in the future?'
❑ 'How will the organisation develop?'
❑ 'I don't expect you to tell me if I've got the job, but could you give me some feedback on how I've come across in this interview? Could you make any suggestions for how I might present myself so that interviewers can make the right decision about me?'

Afterwards

Review the process:

❑ What worked well, and not so well?
❑ What questions gave you trouble?
❑ What extra information would have been useful?
❑ What did the interviewer seem to like and dislike?
❑ What will you do, and *not* do, next time?

Table 7.2 *Main do's and don'ts*

Do	Don't
talk about specific cases, even if asked general questions	rely on opinions or general statements
present yourself positively, getting all your strengths across	waffle, or modestly avoid 'blowing your own trumpet'
work with the interviewer to get the right choice for both	sell yourself aggressively – it puts interviewers off
ask for time to think if you need it	ramble unprepared
go back and rephrase a previous answer if you want to	leave the interviewer with the wrong impression
talk about what you've learned from experience, and how you've developed, and are continuing to develop, skills	give the impression that you believe you 'know it all'
talk about how you've set up and maintained relationships	give the impression that you're a loner (unless that is true and would be an advantage in the job)
talk positively about previous employers, jobs and people	ever complain about others – it's a killer!
try to show that you are choosing the employer as well as the other way round – a good interviewer will credit you for it	give the impression of being desperate for a job, any job – it's another killer!
ask questions about the kind of work, the standards you would be expected to meet, the people you would work with, and anything else that influences whether you would fit in	rush blindly into the first offered job (even if you *are* desperate) without assessing what might go wrong

3: GIVING EFFECTIVE FEEDBACK

Objectives

❑ Develop someone's skills, competence and effectiveness.
❑ Persuade someone to do more of what works well, and less of what doesn't work so well:
   — maintain, reinforce and increase useful behaviours
   — reduce or eliminate unhelpful behaviours.
❑ Communicate a realistic and balanced view of another human being's behaviour.
❑ Communicate honestly and directly, so as to:
   — build effective relationships
   — have mechanisms for tackling and solving problems.
❑ Avoid antagonising the other person.

Note: It is *not* useful to set an objective of changing someone's character or personality. It is almost impossible to do, any attempt will generally worsen relationships, and there are serious ethical considerations. 'You are who you are, but you *can* change what you do.'

Also, this is a crucial skill for managing other people, and most people are *not* good at it. If you doubt this, consider the quality, frequency and balance of the feedback which you get: are all three elements satisfactory?

Preparing

❑ Re-read pages 13–15 and 20–21.
❑ Consider the relationship with the other person:
   — is it your job to develop this person?
   — do you have any other kind of authority to give feedback to the person?
   — if neither of these is true, what will the person feel about getting feedback from you?
❑ You may still want to continue, but should do so with care.

❏ Since feedback will only work if it is seen as balanced and constructive, first define what the person is doing (or not doing) which you consider is useful, helpful or effective.
— be very specific – general praise is useless
— one thing at a time – be realistic
— what evidence do you have for your view? Factual results are very persuasive; unsupported opinions are less persuasive.

❏ Define what the person is doing (or not doing) which you consider is *not* useful, unhelpful or ineffective.
— be very specific – general criticism is useless
— one thing at a time – be realistic
— what evidence do you have for this? Factual results are very persuasive; unsupported opinions are less persuasive.

❏ Consider whether the other person might say either 'I've been doing this for years and nobody ever said anything' or 'You're always nagging me about this'.

❏ How will you create the right circumstances for the other person to be able to accept what you say?
— privacy and confidentiality
— rapport and openness
— no defensiveness on either side.

Getting started

❏ Find a private place, protected from interruptions, where you can be reasonably comfortable and can see and hear one another well.

❏ Make sure your body language is SOLER (see page 27) and your manner is friendly and cooperative (it might be useful to re-read pages 35–42).

❏ Set an objective, as in, 'I'd like to discuss the results we're getting with X'.

❏ Begin with positives and a situation where the person's behaviour got good results and ask:
— 'When you did so-and-so, what effect did it have?'
— 'Was that what you expected?'

— 'Why do you think you got that result?'
— 'Where else could you use a similar approach?'
— 'So what will you do in future?'

❑ Now you can move to a situation where the facts show that the person's behaviour did *not* get good results, and ask the same thing, adding:
— 'What else could you do that would be more likely to get the result you want?' You may need to get several possibilities, by asking 'And what else?' until you get an answer which you can support.

Table 7.3 *Main do's and don'ts*

Do	Don't
consider how to make your feedback acceptable to the other person – everyone gets defensive if they feel criticised	impose your views
concentrate on what people do, and so can change	criticise someone's personality, which is hard to change
remember that what you do (and how you do it) will affect how the other reacts and promote (or damage) cooperation	demonise the other by blaming them for everything
be specific and detailed by discussing particular cases	generalise, as in 'You always . . .', 'You never . . .'
base discussion on some observable results so that you can agree that a particular set of behaviours does (or does not) produce specified results	attack someone's behaviour without facts and evidence
get the other person to describe results and behaviour by asking them	deliver your opinions as if they were the last word

questions about what actually happened

stay friendly, reasonable and calm | attack, put down or bully the other person

give as much positive as negative feedback (or even more) | be destructive by only giving the unbalanced negative

make your positive feedback as detailed as your negative | just say 'You're doing all right, really, but . . .' and follow this with a long catalogue of complaint

ask the other person to work out how to use the useful behaviours more, and what to do instead of the behaviours that are not producing good results | say 'If I were you . . .', which means 'If I were you (which I'm not), I think I would have done it this way (which you didn't) but I didn't actually have to face what you did (so I might have done something different)'

concentrate on one set of behaviours at a time, and pick only behaviours that really affect results | overload people by dumping large amounts of feedback on them, some of it trivial

spend most of the time discussing things to do, as this leads to solutions | spend most of the time discussing what has been done, as this cannot be changed and tends to generate arguments

talk less than the other person | monopolise the conversation

give feedback as soon as possible after the event | save it all up until you have amassed a steaming heap, as this will make it harder for you to keep your temper

Ending effectively

Since the objective is to develop people by getting them to do more of what works, the ending should concentrate on what the person is actually going to do.

❏ Invite the other person to summarise:
  — what's been discussed
  — what the person is doing that works well
  — what the person is doing that works less well
  — what the person will do in future to make more use of what works and to use alternatives to what works less well
  — what you are going to do to help
  — what you haven't been able to agree, if anything.
❏ Add anything to this summary if you feel you must.
❏ Consider asking the other person to write down the actions and then take a copy – this is better than you making notes.
❏ Agree when you will next meet to discuss the results of the actions you are both going to take.

Afterwards

Review the process.

❏ What worked well, and not so well?
❏ What will you do, and *not* do, next time?

Meet to review what has happened and to discuss what else you might both do.

4: COPING WITH FEEDBACK

Objectives

❏ Develop your skills, competence and effectiveness.
❏ Learn how to do more of what works well, and less of what doesn't work so well:
 — maintain, reinforce and increase useful behaviours
 — reduce or eliminate unhelpful behaviours.
❏ Discover a realistic and balanced view of your behaviour.
❏ Communicate honestly and directly, so as to:
 — build effective relationships
 — have mechanisms for tackling and solving problems.
❏ Avoid antagonising the other person.

Preparing

This is a crucial skill, but most people are *not* good at it. Expect the other person to be unhappy about giving feedback, and perhaps therefore clumsy or defensive. Decide that *you* will not be defensive, whatever happens, but will learn something useful every time. This is particularly important if you feel you have been attacked without warning – the other person may have been saving up the feedback, but have finally snapped.

If you get notice of a feedback session:

❏ review the results you are satisfied with, and consider what you did that worked;
❏ review the results you are dissatisfied with, where some other action might have produced a better result, and consider what else you might have done.

Consider initiating a feedback session by asking the other person:

❏ 'What do you feel I'm doing that works – in detail, please?'
❏ 'What do you feel I'm doing that *doesn't* work – in detail, please?'

Prepare to concentrate on:

❏ the facts of particular cases;

❏ what you can do to get better results, both by increasing effective behaviours and decreasing ineffective ones.

Getting started

If you feel suddenly attacked by unexpected negative feedback, slow down the pace to give time to think.

❏ Say 'I can see that this is important, and we obviously need to discuss it'.
❏ Suggest moving to somewhere private.
❏ Ask detailed questions to show you are taking the feedback seriously, like:
— 'Can you go over the facts for me?'
— 'What has happened to make you feel this?'
— 'What do you believe I did?'
— 'What else is important?'
— 'What do you feel I should have done?'
❏ When you have a clear picture of what the person is saying and why they are saying it, summarise what you've heard, factually and undefensively. This will defuse any negative emotions that the other person has.
❏ Begin a planned feedback session by following the lead of the person who is giving you feedback.
❏ As soon as you can, ask:
— 'Can we agree that we both want to solve any problems or disagreements between us?'
— If this works, continue with the problem-solving process described on pages 20–21.

Ending effectively

Since the objective is to develop by doing more of what works, the ending should concentrate on what both of you are actually going to do.

Offer to summarise:

❏ what's been discussed;
❏ what you are doing that works well;

Table 7.4 *Main do's and don'ts*

Do	Don't
treat feedback as an opportunity to learn something useful	be defensive
listen to what the other person has to say – they're entitled to their opinions, and you're entitled to yours	argue or 'Yes, but . . .'
try to get some balance into the discussion by asking for positives while also accepting how the other person feels about the negatives	be afraid to ask for positive feedback
concentrate on working out and agreeing things you can do to improve your effectiveness and your results	get side-tracked into pointless arguments about what you, or somebody else, did or didn't do
try to keep the discussion about observable facts and cases	get drawn into generalities
stay friendly, reasonable and calm	put yourself in the wrong by losing control

❏ what you are doing that works less well;
❏ what you will do in future to make more use of what works; and to use alternatives to what works less well;
❏ what you would like the other person to do to help;
❏ what you haven't been able to agree, if anything.

If this offer is refused, ask the other person to summarise.

❏ Agree who will write down the actions and make a copy for both of you.
❏ Agree when you will next meet to discuss the results of the actions you are both going to take.

Afterwards

Review the process.

❑ What worked well, and not so well?
❑ What will you do, and *not* do, next time?

Meet to review what has happened and to discuss what else you might both do.

5: RUNNING A MEETING

Objectives

❑ Communicate information between everyone in a group.
❑ Make sure people agree:
— what the meeting is for, and what its objectives are
— what the rules are for the meeting
— how long the meeting will take.
❑ Maintain unbiased and unprejudiced control of the meeting.
❑ Make sure all relevant facts and opinions are expressed.
❑ Get the paperwork right.
❑ See that the meeting:
— keeps to time and on the point
— resolves any conflicts
— agrees realistic, relevant and practical decisions
— is accurately recorded.

Preparing

It is best to have an agenda, as the meeting will otherwise have to spend time setting an agenda at the start.
Agendas should:

❑ stipulate *Who, When* and *Where*;
❑ reach people in time for them to prepare.

A good agenda item states:

❑ *what* is to be discussed, *what* the objective is, *why* this is being done and *when* results are expected:
— 'Review specifications for the new drive and agree a budget for this year so as to brief contractors by 1st May'.

This allows people to prepare properly, which in turn allows you to *require* people to prepare, thus saving time and trouble.

❑ Familiarise yourself with each topic so that you can brief the meeting helpfully.

❑ If there is a meeting secretary, some of this work can be shared.

Getting started

Begin by reviewing and getting agreement from everyone as to:

❑ what the meeting is for, and what its objectives are;
❑ what the rules are for the meeting;
❑ how long the meeting will take;
❑ how long you will devote to each topic.

If there was no agenda in advance, agree one now. Consider posting on a flip chart or board:
❑ the overall objective of the meeting;
❑ the time you will finish;
❑ the topics you will discuss;
❑ the time you will devote to each topic, basing this on how important it is – more important topics get a longer time.

Doing this makes it easier to control time and keep people to the point.

Brief the meeting on the first topic (*Tip: be brief!*) Give the background and history; the objective of discussing it now; and how long is given to this topic.

For this and subsequent topics, elicit the new facts people have and summarise these. Don't allow opinions or disagreements until all the facts are known.

Now elicit opinions:

❑ look for agreements and summarise these;
❑ ask silent people for their views;
❑ try to remain impartial, friendly and calm;
❑ don't permit personal attacks;
❑ keep people on the point by restating the objective;
❑ keep people on time by reminding them of the time allocated to the topic.

Finally:

❑ summarise the main agreements and disagreements;

❑ seek decisions and actions to move matters forward (if action is irrelevant or impossible then close the discussion);

❑ summarise and record decisions.

Table 7.5 *Main do's and don'ts*

Do	Don't
remain impartial, unbiased, reasonable and friendly	abuse your power by imposing a decision
use meetings for everyone to communicate	cheat by pretending to consult when you have already decided what you are going to tell people to do. You have the right to use whatever authority you have to order people; you will lose respect if you pretend that you are really doing something else
make sure that you are well briefed and prepared	let unreadiness sabotage your control of the meeting
set time limits and make sure people observe these	allow meetings to drift or overrun
start on time; people will learn that if they want to influence decisions they must be punctual	wait for people who are late – this simply tells them that it will be all right to keep you waiting next time, too
insist that people prepare properly for the meeting	allow people to be lazy and catch up during the meeting's valuable time
keep people on the point by summarising and reminding them of the objectives and the timing	allow people to waste time by rambling, by introducing side issues, by reopening issues already decided, or by being unprepared for the discussion

keep looking for points of agreement and summarising these	allow people to spend all the time disagreeing
keep looking for decisions and practical things to do	let a meeting end without agreeing to do *something*
make sure that quieter, less noisy people get a hearing	let one or two people dominate
adjourn if things are getting out of hand, asking everyone 'to return in thirty minutes with practical proposals for moving us forward from this disagreement so that we don't get stuck for ever'	let people bang on repeating their uncompromising positions
stick to the agenda that people have prepared for	let people introduce their last-minute thoughts under the guise of 'Any Other Business', as this is a notorious time-waster. Schedule the item for next meeting
make sure that the minutes record decisions and actions	try to keep a verbatim record of discussions

Ending effectively

❏ Summarise points of agreement and disagreement, decisions reached and, actions agreed, with *Who* will do *What* by *When*.

❏ Thank people for their efforts.

❏ Agree time, place and skeleton agenda for the next meeting.

Afterwards

Review the process.

❏ What worked well, and not so well?

❏ What will you do, and *not* do, next time?

❏ Monitor what happens as a result of the actions.

6: CONTRIBUTING EFFECTIVELY TO A MEETING

Objectives

❏ Listen and learn from others
❏ Be heard and influence others
❏ Reach decisions when this is relevant
❏ Keep the meeting to the point and as short as possible.

Preparing

❏ If there is an agenda, read it; if there is no agenda, find out what the objective and coverage of the meeting is to be.
❏ Do your homework:
— review what you know of the topic
— decide what you want to learn at the meeting
— define what result you want from the meeting.
❏ Set yourself to help the meeting:
— achieve its objective
— keep to time
— keep on the point
— achieve your objective.
❏ Gather facts, evidence or documents that you need to take.

Getting started

If there is no agenda, ask for:

❏ the objective and coverage of the meeting
❏ how long it is to take
❏ what topics will be discussed and how long each topic is to be.

Ending effectively

If the chair does not summarise:

❏ points of agreement and disagreement
❏ decisions reached

Table 7.6 *Main do's and don'ts*

Do	Don't
listen to what others say and consider it	just defend your corner against all comers
speak when you can promote your case or help the meeting to progress in some way	speak when you have nothing in particular to say
keep all your contributions brief, clear, and to the point	ramble, waffle, drift off the point or keep repeating the same view
make sure you have heard all the facts before you start to give your opinions	smear egg on your own face by jumping in on the basis of inadequate evidence
sit where you catch the Chair's eye and move forward when you want to do it, so that you can be heard	sit where the Chair cannot see you, or suffer in silence
check you understand critical points by summarising them	disagree with someone without first checking that you have correctly understood what they said
help more silent members to contribute	hog the limelight
'label' what you are doing: 'Can I add to John's idea . . .'; 'I'd like to propose . . .'; 'Can I check I've got this right . . .?'	leave people to guess what you are up to
ask the Chair to summarise if this is not happening	abdicate your duty to help the meeting
agree your fair share of the actions	cop out of doing something you agreed to do

❏ actions agreed, with *Who* will do *What* by *When* and agree time, place and skeleton agenda for the next meeting, then ask for these.

Afterwards

❏ Do what you agreed to do
❏ Review the process:
— What worked well, and not so well?
— What will you do, and *not* do, next time?

SOURCES AND FURTHER READING

It has been suggested that 'an expert is somebody who's read more than one book on the subject.' Here are some of the books that have influenced this one.

Argyle, Michael and Henderson, Monika (1985) *The Anatomy of Relationships*, Penguin, London.

Black, Roger (1987) *Getting Things Done*, Michael Joseph, London.

Chapman, Elwood N (1989) *Improving Relations at Work*, Kogan Page, London.

Edelman, Robert J (1993) *Interpersonal Conflicts at Work*, BPS Books.

Fisher, Roger and Ury, William (1981, 1986) *Getting to Yes*, Hutchinson Business Books, London.

Fletcher, John (1973, 1988) *Effective Interviewing*, Kogan Page, London.

Guirdham, Maureen (1990) *Interpersonal Skills At Work*, Prentice Hall.

Honey, Peter (1988, 1993) *Improve Your People Skills*, IPM, London.

Jay, Anthony (1972) *Effective Presentation*, BIM, London.

Lloyd, Sam R (1988) *How to Develop Assertiveness*, Kogan Page, London.

McMillan, Sandy (1985) *Stand Up and Talk!*, Postlip Press.

Martin, David M (1993) *Tough Talking*, Pitman Publishing, London.

Nelson-Jones, Richard (1986) *Human Relationship Skills*, Cassell, London.

Peel, Malcolm (1995) *Improving Your Communication Skills*, Kogan Page, London.

Roberts, Celia (1985) *The Interview Game*, BBC Books, London.

Semler, Ricardo (1993) *Maverick!*, Arrow Books, London.

Shea, Michael (1993, 1994) *Personal Impact*, Mandarin, London.

Skynner, Robin and Cleese, John (1993) *Life And How To Survive It*, Methuen, London.

Stanton, Nicki (1982, 1986, 1995) *The Business of Communicating*, Macmillan Education (Breakthrough), London.

Stewart, Valerie and Stewart, Andrew (1982, 1988) *Managing The Poor Performer*, Wildwood House, Aldershot.

INDEX